ART OF THE
HOT ROD

KEN GROSS
PHOTOGRAPHY BY PETER HARHOLDT
FOREWORD BY ALEX XYDIAS

CRESTLINE

© 2012 Motorbooks
Text © 2008, 2012 Ken Gross
Photography © 2008, 2012 Peter Harholdt

This edition published in 2020 by Crestline,
an imprint of The Quarto Group
142 West 36th Street, 4th Floor
New York, NY 10018 USA
T (212) 779-4972 **F** (212) 779-6058
www.QuartoKnows.com

First published in 2008 by Motorbooks, an imprint of The Quarto Group,
100 Cummings Center, Suite 265-D, Beverly, MA 01915, USA.

Crestline titles are also available at discount for retail, wholesale, promotional, and bulk purchase. For details, contact the Special Sales Manager by email at specialsales@quarto.com or by mail at The Quarto Group, Attn: Special Sales Manager, 100 Cummings Center, Suite 265-D, Beverly, MA 01915, USA.

To find out more about our books, visit us online at www.motorbooks.com.

10 9 8 7 6 5 4 3 2 1

ISBN: 978-0-7858-3848-7

Editor: Peter Schletty, Darwin Holmstrom
Design Manager: James Kegley
Layout: Melissa Khaira

Cover designer: Claire MacMasters

Printed in Singapore COS122019

About the Author

An automobile and motorcycle enthusiast since childhood, Ken Gross was executive director of the Petersen Automotive Museum, in Los Angeles, California, for five years following a career in advertising and marketing. His car, travel, and motorcycle writing has appeared in *Robb Report*, *The Rodder's Journal*, *Automobile Magazine*, and *Road & Track*. Ken and his wife, Patricia Serratore, live in Hamilton, Virginia, with their children, Jake and Kayla.

About the Photographer

Peter Harholdt is a lifelong car enthusiast, SCCA racer, and preeminent studio photographer. He has been entrusted to photograph countless priceless works of art for museums and exhibit catalogs. He has developed a portable studio that allows him to create portraits of hot rods in any environment or locale.

Front cover photo © Peter Harholdt.

On the frontispiece: Front grille of Barry Lobeck's red '32 coupe.

On the title pages: *Extremeliner* by Ken "POSIES" Fenical.

CONTENTS

HOT ROD SHOPS, THEN AND NOW
By Alex Xydias, So-Cal Speed Shop Founder

I started my Hot Rod shop right after I got out of the Army Air Corps in 1946. But we never did any customizing there. I became aware of customizing because Jimmy Summers was located right across from Fairfax High School, and I'd go over there and watch him do stuff. At that time there weren't a lot of shops doing this sort of work. Jimmy Summers and George Duvall were two of the best-known guys before the war.

Jimmy had a guy working for him named Bob Fairman . . . they called him "Barbells." He built a chopped '36 Ford and ran the front fenders all the way back in fadeaway style, like the Buicks of that era. His was the first custom I'd ever seen that did that. He took the door handles off and put a toe opener under the door. What a beautiful car that was. I've never seen pictures of it in any of the magazines.

I vividly recall the first time I took my '34 Ford cabriolet to Glen Houser's Carson Top Shop. That was like going into a giant car show. The cars sitting there were all so beautifully done. The last thing guys generally did was get that Carson padded top. The cars all had sunken license plates and smoothed noses; it was a wonderful experience to go there.

Their turnaround was fast. Cars came in on Monday and Tuesday, and they were finished on Thursday or Friday. It was about a week, and boy, that was like waiting forever. Once you'd saved up the money to do it, you couldn't wait for it to be done. I don't remember what it cost, but for those days it required most of us to save money for it. That was expensive by the normal standards.

Before the war, the big thing for both hot rod guys and the customizers was putting on hydraulic brakes and installing '40 Ford transmission column shifts. When I opened my shop, customizing was starting up just like the hot rod business, but we didn't get along with those guys; we didn't really understand them or know them. Many of them became hot rodders because they needed power for those cars, so they bought parts from me. But I didn't know a lot of early custom guys. George Barris and I didn't get to know each other for a long time.

I felt Jimmy Summers was the top customizer and car builder before the war. He did some remarkable things in his small shop, including building those solid rear fenders for my '34 cabriolet. After the war, many of my customers, like Dean Batchelor and Keith Baldwin, became my good friends. They were all Valley guys, so the Valley Custom Shop is where they went. And I got to know the shop owners, Neil Emory and Clay Jensen.

Compared to the present, nobody's shop was very big in those days. I'm sure you've seen the old picture of Barris' shop, with the two chopped Merc's out in front of it. That was about what everybody had. Valley Custom was a little place and so was So-Cal. We were all just starting out.

But they sure got the work done. Neil Emory built the streamlined headrest for me for the So-Cal Belly Tank. He told me later on that it was his first real job that required bending metal and shaping it. Before that he did sunken license plates, and some nosing and decking, but he hadn't really gotten into chopped tops. Making that headrest (which, incidentally, really helped the looks of that car) showed he had a little flair. Today that headrest still stands out; it's one of the visual highlights of the car.

Doane Spencer worked in my shop for a short time installing a V-8/60 in an MG TC. It took a long time, and then he moved on and worked on his own. Ray Brown hadn't quite started yet; he was still working at Eddie Meyer's shop in West Hollywood, and they mainly just did engines. So did Vic Edelbrock Sr., Ak Miller, and Earl Evans. Vic just had a three or four-stall gas station over on Highland Avenue. All his machines were practically out in the parking lot. His little teeny office was probably four feet by four feet. Edelbrock didn't have room to do much of anything until he moved to Jefferson Avenue. Then his new building looked just enormous to us. It was like a cavern in the back. That's where they put the dyno. They were building engines for the Pierson Brothers, Don Towle, and us. And they built midget racers.

We never thought Vic would ever fill that building up; but as his business grew, it soon became too small. And that's the way it was, years later, when the new So-Cal shop started in Pomona, but Pete Chapouris and his gang quickly filled it up, building new cars and restoring hot rods.

Looking back, George DuVall was at Southern California Plating. He came up with that split windshield design that Doane used on his roadster, and people are still using on their cars. Racecar builder Frank Kurtis was over in Glendale, and he made this "step-up" midget body. It was a real advancement that was just so much better looking than anyone had ever run before, much the way the L.A. guys like Watson and Epperly did later with their Offy roadsters at Indianapolis.

Kurtis-Kraft was not very far from Ed Winfield's place, so when I'd go over to Winfield's to pick up some camshafts I'd just stand and marvel at what those guys were doing. Cars that were once awkward-looking were becoming beautiful. And guys were starting to understand and implement aerodynamics—that happened at Bonneville, too. Our So-Cal streamliner, built at Valley Custom Shop, was certainly a step up.

And now, when I look at all the hot rod shops doing business, I think the quality of their work is amazing. I don't know how many guys were really doing that quality of work or whether they were just kind of getting by. Maybe they didn't have the equipment or the training and they were doing it all on their own, and learning as they went. It was, "Let's try to chop this car," and then "Oh my God, we got into something here that we never knew was so difficult." Cars were pretty cheap then. Maybe they could start all over with another Mercury.

The sophistication and creativity that these guys have today is incredible. I'm stunned at how Pete Chapouris can walk up to a stock car and see immediately what's wrong with it, even the best cars. And they're all that way. I visited Dave Simard's place near Boston and saw what great work he was doing out in the backwoods. And Roy Brizio's work is marvelous. These guys are getting great reputations. I admire them all . . . not only for their skill, but for their imagination and creativity.

Like that '36 Ford coupe that Troy did for the Ridler Award—I was walking through the Grand National Show on the way to our So-Cal booth, and I stopped dead in my tracks to look at that car, primarily because of the color. I hadn't even had a chance to look closely at the car, but the color struck me. Later I told Troy that the color, and of course the car, mechanically, was unbelievable.

And we build those at So-Cal, too. Pete and Silky and Jimmy have this incredible talent. We recently built a cement pumper that's one of the best-looking custom things ever, and all it really does is pump cement. This guy came in and said, "We've got this big cement show in Las Vegas. Guys are starting to customize these pumps, along with the trucks that tow them. And I want you to do one for me." So they came up with a great cement pumper that looks like a hot rod, with louvers on the sides, chromed wheels, and a 100-point paint job. It shows that customizing is really far-reaching today.

In the early days, almost all the hot rod shops were located in Southern California. It all grew out of that small nucleus. I'm so glad I happened to be part of that era, where I could see it all evolve. But we really didn't realize the potential. We'd never have thought it could grow like it did and become what it is today

Of course, I had to learn, and then I really appreciated how diversified all these guys were, all around the country. I just couldn't believe how quickly they caught up—we did have quite a lead—and how quickly they became very well known. I remember, years ago, when we were shaking our heads at this guy, Don Garlits, and his "Swamp Rat." We figured all the clocks in Florida had to be fast. Of course, when he came out to Bakersfield, he blew everybody off. It took us a long time to get over that. I'm not sure I'm over it yet. I'm still used to thinking that Southern California is the tops.

Perhaps when *Art of the Hot Rod* comes out, I'll finally get it through my head. The names in this book are just amazing. There's not a corner of this country that doesn't have somebody who can do a 100-point car.

Just turn the page and you'll see.

—Alex Xydias, March 2008

Acknowledgments and Introduction

Nobody knows where the term *hot rod* originated. The best explanation is that it may be a contraction of the term "hot roadster," because open two-seaters defined the genre in the sport's formative years. Attempts to explain the term "hot rod" remind me of the judge who insisted he couldn't *define* pornography but said, "I know it when I see it."

It all started with stripped-down, souped-up, older cars built by young men who possessed some or all of the skills required to modify engines and restyle bodies (and often raced what they built). Over time, hot rods evolved into highly sophisticated creations. They lacked even a single standardized part and were powered by state-of-the-art engines with many times their original power.

Nearly a century has passed since guys in Ford Model Ts with RAJO heads raced each other on the streets and dry lake beds. Hot rodding, at first an outlaw sport, soon policed itself, established governing bodies and racing associations, then spun in countless new directions, with acclaimed heroes, culture and rules, a few taboos, and even its own language. But very few basic elements have changed.

And we know it when we see it.

Art of the Hot Rod celebrates mechanical wizardry and extraordinary craftsmanship. It encourages personalized styles, lauds clever component switching, rewards invention, and thrives on the creation of new visual elements and fresh approaches to old problems.

And it's still about speed and performance.

For every step forward, there's a step back. Today's traditionalists and rat rod/retro-rod enthusiasts build cars that resemble rides from the '40s and '50s. The rise of an enormous aftermarket industry has meant that the average hot rodder—the guy with very little money and few basic skills—can assemble a decent car that reflects his dreams. In contrast, wealthy enthusiasts, the so-called "checkbook rodders," bankroll big-name builders with unlimited budgets, resulting in creations that rival OEM auto show concept cars for fit, finish, and yes, dramatic presence.

But it wasn't always that way.

Rods and customs flourished first in Los Angeles, then spread rapidly cross-country, propelled by the rise of dedicated monthlies like *Hot Rod* magazine, *Hop Up*, and *Rod & Custom*. Hot rodding was largely a workingman's pastime. Few people had the money to commission a custom build. Thanks to military service training and high school shop courses, some guys possessed most skills needed to build an entire car, and/or they traded abilities. A machinist would do the engine work for a friend who could paint, and have his car refinished in return. Hot rod club members helped one another. If you couldn't build your own car, or most of it, you weren't considered a real hot rodder.

Half a century ago, only a few shops worked exclusively on hot rods. Whitey Clayton and the Ayala Brothers, Gil and Al, created the Eddie Dye roadster; Clay Jensen and Neil Emory's Valley Custom Shop helped Dick Flint build his stunning '29. Dr. Leland Wetzel's channeled '32 roadster was the work of George and Sam Barris.

Custom cars usually demanded more fabrication skill than hot rods. The earliest celebrated practitioners, Harry Westergard and Jimmy Summers, began as skilled body and fender men. Especially in California, demand for custom work and widespread magazine exposure permitted the best of the breed to concentrate profitably on restyling. The custom car phenomenon soon spread eastward to Clarkaiser and the Alexander Brothers in Detroit and Frank Marratta in Connecticut. East Coast customs were no less plentiful, but major magazine coverage was West Coast–centric, so they weren't as well known.

It's rare now for any single person to possess all the skills needed to produce a trendsetting feature car or a major show winner. Coveted trophies like the San Francisco Rod Custom and Motorcycle Show's (née Oakland) Don Ridler Award and the Grand National Roadster Show's AMBR (America's Most Beautiful Roadster) celebrate professional builders (and their crews) as much as the cars.

But big awards aren't the only way to keep score. Many stunning cars never become magazine or TV features. A great effort from a small shop can still set a trend. You have to seek these guys out. Thanks to still-vibrant hot rodding magazines, national associations like the National Street Rod Association (NSRA) and Goodguys, with huge shows and extensive websites, on-line resources like the HAMB message board and Hot Rod Hotline, and the phenomenon of TV docu-dramas that celebrate hot rodding, word travels fast. A single feature appearance can make a builder a star. If his car wins the AMBR or the Ridler, he's even hotter.

But staying hot takes talent. And that's what inspired this book. We're celebrating the consummate artistry of 20 varied rod and custom shops, large and small. Each takes a somewhat different approach, some have become involved in historic hot rod restorations, but they all have common qualities: These shop owners and their associates are highly imaginative, immensely skilled, and, not surprisingly, never satisfied. Just as artists have done for decades, they accept commissions and build (you could say paint or sculpt) original works for their clients (you could even say patrons). While they take justifiable pride in their creations, most will tell you their favorite car is the one they'll build next. Acknowledged as some of the most talented artists in a crowded field, they're a relatively recent phenomenon.

Peter Harholdt and I are proud to present them in this book.

A talented visual artist himself, Peter did the heavy lifting. Crisscrossing the country, towing his ingenious home-built portable photo studio, he spent long (and often hot) summer days with each builder, painstakingly photographing their shops, their best cars, and the builders themselves. And he did a fabulous job. Peter's meticulous work perfectly captures the genius of our featured craftsmen.

I can't thank him enough for including me in this project.

Completing *Art of the Hot Rod* took longer than we'd originally planned. Both Peter and I were ill at separate times (we're fine now!), which necessitated several delays. For my part, I want to sincerely thank Chris McCreary and Chris Shelton, two talented writers, formerly with *The Rodder's Journal* and *Street Rodder* magazine, for helping with interviews and chapter drafts during a time when I was simply unable to function. Without their skill and creativity, this book would not have been completed.

I especially want to thank each of the builders for making their precious time available for Peter, and for speaking with me and my two associates. Although several of these guys are household names, and a few are still just under the national radar, many know one another personally (or they know of each other). It was a compliment to hear that the builders we selected liked the concept of this book and were pleased to be recognized. They are sculptors with sheet metal, magicians with motors, paragons of paint, and, well, you get the idea.

More importantly, thanks to the work of these builders and their shops, the art of the hot rod remains vibrant, creative, and forever evolving.

If you need any more proof, just turn the page . . .

—Ken Gross

An art historian setting out to show the connections between art and machinery would probably begin with Leonardo da Vinci's machine drawings. There would also be a mention of Ettore Bugatti's time in art school prior to his long career as designer and builder, a quote from Filippo Tommaso Marinetti's futurist manifesto, and possibly a reference to Marcel Duchamp's mechanisms. For our project, however, we fast-forward to the United States just after World War II.

In that postwar period, there was rapid development in art forms that are uniquely American: the abstract expressionist movement followed by pop art, in music the advent of bebop in jazz along with the invention and proliferation of rock and roll, in literature the radical new voices of Allen Ginsberg and Jack Kerouac, and for us car enthusiasts, the explosion of activity in hot rodding. Tom Wolfe, an authority on our culture, called these car builders "America's true avant-garde." In all of these cases, the new work, although rooted in history, was revolutionary.

Having spent decades in painters' and sculptors' studios, jazz clubs, and car builders' shops, I find the same sort of creative drive, open-mindedness, ambition, and restless energy. Spending time with Ken Fenical, Zane Cullen, or Troy Trepanier has a feel similar to time spent with Henry Moore, Jules Olitski, Kiki Smith, or Elvin Jones.

For my part, I grew up in both worlds with engineers, writers, painters, sculptors, and musicians. There was never a feeling of crossing over from one discipline to another. It made perfect sense that my first racecar was built in my studio at art school. My work in *Art of the Hot Rod* is one more confluence of these experiences.

In photographing the cars for this book, I take the same visual approach as I do for precious objects in museum collections. First, I isolate the object in the frame and do not make it a single element in a larger landscape. Second, I make it tangible and find a real sense of the material, the paint, the chrome, the leather, and in some cases, the rust. Third, I single out

signature design elements that can stand on their own. Overall, my goal is to make the photography (and the photographer) disappear. To make the objects seem to illuminate themselves. To establish a direct connection between the viewer and the object. To entice the viewer to touch the page.

It was the generation before mine and Ken Gross' that was at the center of the movement. For the most part, the builders in this book are boomers, too, the second wave of hot rodders who picked up where the pioneers had stopped. When I began the photography sessions with these twenty builders, I expected to find virtuoso designers and fabricators among them, the guys in my generation. I wasn't disappointed. Every one of them is passionate about his work. There was a surprise, however, in the next generation. At almost every shop are young guys who have amazing skill and imagination. If you have fears of the traditions dying out, don't worry. The future is in talented hands.

In addition to this book's twenty builders and everyone in their shops, I would like to thank the following:

Our sequence of editors at MBI who initiated and have seen this project through. Each has made a contribution.

Ken Gross, who is encyclopedic on everything automotive and is great fun to work with. I am looking forward to the sequel.

Alex Xydias for writing our foreword. I had a more powerful sense of history sitting in the So-Cal coupe than from walking through Monticello.

Don Schnieders, who collaborated on the concept of the mobile studio and did design and fabrication through its several iterations.

Chuck Andersen, who has been my coach through the transition from film to digital photography. Chuck is able to troubleshoot equipment issues from across oceans or continents.

Donna Tribby, who assisted every day from the first builder on, and to daughter Tara Lawrence, an experienced and capable studio assistant, who joined us on the West Coast and worked the third half lap of the country.

To my late father, Dick Harholdt, who shared his appreciation and understanding of machinery with me. As a child, the bedtime stories I heard weren't fairy tales, they were detailed descriptions of the way things work. Four cycles, two cycles, diesels (Gee, Dad, no spark plugs?), everything to do with cars, heavy equipment, aircraft, etc. He took me to my first circle track race at six, road race at twelve, and as a bonus, the construction company he managed built the local drag strip. Free passes!

Thanks again, Dad.

—Peter Harholdt

CHAPTER 1

DAVE SIMARD
Driven to Perfection

At East Coast Custom, in Leominster, Massachusetts, 40 miles west of Boston, Dave Simard turns out beautifully-detailed, well-engineered, award-winning street rods and historic hot rod restorations. Along with his two capable associates, Mark Szymt and Stan Decoste, Simard works on every car in the shop himself. *That's* the big attraction. He is immensely skilled, his knowledge of early Ford mechanicals and body parts is encyclopedic, and he's a perfectionist. It doesn't come any better.

A former mechanical engineer turned metal-working wizard, Simard chopped tops part-time, developing his skills, before he opened his shop in 1981. "You have to restore a car first," he believes, "before making a hot rod out of it. If you don't, you lose all the reference points. You need to *maintain* those reference points, or you constantly dig yourself a deeper hole. You're cutting things to fix gaps, but you don't know if you're cutting the right or the wrong thing." So he sets up each chassis, with the body

mounted, making sure everything is true *before* he starts cutting.

Using finely honed metal-finishing techniques, never resorting to filler, Simard ensures panels are arrow-straight and correct from side to side. Simard takes extraordinary steps to make sure all his cars are perfectly aligned. "When you use original '32 parts, you have to start somewhere," he says. "We start at the back. You get the door lined up with the rear quarter, then you get the front of the door lined up to the cowl, by adjusting the body through cutting, welding, or shimming. Once the hood is fitted and the body is bolted on, then you do the hood and the grille, and they have to be done jointly. You want the beltline on the money."

And his are. Henry Ford never built a '32, '33, '34 roadster or coupe the way they come out of Simard's shop. Even though we're used to a much higher standard today, Simard takes it even higher. On the period-perfect Deuce roadster he built for me in the late '90s, you can slide a piece of welding rod

through *any* hood, door, or trunk gap, and they're all alike, all perfect. Simard has a great eye for proportion, and an appreciation for authentic hot rod history. My car was picked as one of the top 75 '32 Fords of all time. The five-year build process was like having your best friend build your car. By the end, Simard and I could finish each other's sentences. That's the only kind of relationship you want with a builder.

Simard's shop restored the ex–Jim Khougaz dry lakes racing '32 (another top-75 car) for Dr. Mark Van Buskirk, literally from a pile of parts that had been stored in Khougaz's balancing shop attic for decades. "We did a few things differently," Simard recalls. "When everything arrived, I thought, 'I really should put this car together, with all the original pieces, to better evaluate what we'd have to do.' So we did, then we took plenty of pictures. Our biggest challenge was that the body is actually welded to the chassis in front, so we had to paint it, then weld it back together perfectly—there could be no adjustments— then we repainted the areas that were blistered by the welding. Next we painted the complete body and carefully welded it and the chassis together. It had to be perfect, so the doors, hood, radiator, and grille would fit just right. There was no second chance to adjust anything."

The Khougaz Deuce features an exquisite, hand-formed and louvered aluminum belly pan. The original was too far gone for anything but a pattern. "We must have over 400 hours in fabricating a new one," Simard says. "It was a lot of work." The finished result is the crowning touch on the aerodynamic little roadster and helped it earn the coveted Bruce Meyer Preservation Award at the 2003 Grand National Roadster Show.

Simard's expertise with early Fords stems in part from his passionate collecting of cars and rare parts. He understands the important eras, especially the '40s, '50s, and '60s, and knows, with the studied skill of a museum curator, how not to mix pieces from one period to the next.

Many times when we needed a special old part for my car, Simard would offer it up from his personal stash. He keeps this treasure trove off to one side, away from the hammering and leadwork, in a long, barn-like structure. As you enter, a pile of original chassis rises like a stack of bedframes. Overhead, in the rafters, are fenders, hood sides, dashes, and decklids. Peering further in the dim light, you see car after car, parked so closely together they resemble one of those hand-held puzzles where you have to move nearly every plastic square before you can align each one in order. Most are black or in primer; not one is show-car finished. A few customer cars await their turn. Way in back, you can make out a couple of chopped fifties customs, several musclecars, and a pickup or two.

Every car has a story. A few of them are runners. But many aren't, and that's fine. Simard owns nearly all of them, and he has plans for each one. In between customer cars, he works on his own. Nothing's really for sale, and yet, if an opportunity comes along, who knows? Simard likes to keep cars, but he trades and upgrades as he rebuilds.

Simard may have a plan for everything, but he's in no particular hurry. You could say he enjoys just *possessing* these artifacts as much as he does working on them, and that's true regardless of whether they're ever finished. Simard epitomizes the persistent collector gene that lurks deep inside us all. He's built up his collection through clever horse trading, keeping his ear to the ground for opportunities, combing swap meets, and a bit of luck.

"I have all this stuff because I like it," he says. "You develop a preference for a particular body style like a '34 three-window. You build *that* car (which he did), then you look at '32–'34's with other body styles and think, 'Boy, I'd love to have a '32 roadster or a '32 three-window.' If and when the right car comes along, you acquire it. And you think, 'Down the road I'm going do something with this car.'

"Whether you *ever* get to it or not isn't as important as the *dream* of having the car come true, so you go to bed at night and you, think, 'That three-window would really look good if I had, *this* engine in it with *these* wheels and tires, or that roadster would look good with this combination.' I've collected cars, over many years, thinking, I'll hold on to most of 'em, and hopefully I'll do something with 'em.'"

Simard also hoards decent pieces. "If you see a good part you think you can use, like a door or a deck-lid, you buy it for projects down the road because, as you're thinking about all these different cars and how you're going to build them, you remember parts you need and try to get them when you can." He makes a cross-country trip each year to do just that.

For Simard, "'32 to '34 Fords just define 'hot rod.' Everybody who's been into hot rods relates to them. Just look at that grille . . . *that's* a hot rod. So many great magazine articles evolved around them. Of course there were Ts, As, and '40s, but the core cars have always been from 1932 to '34. Take any Deuce and pull the fenders off, throw the running boards away, and you instantly have a hot rod. That's what happened in the '30s, and it's stayed that way."

Simard's always had hot rods, but he's also liked '60s cars and musclecars. Then, as time went on, he became disenchanted. "I started getting rid of some of the other cars when I realized that rather than having say, a '65 Chevelle, I'd rather have another '32 roadster."

"I still have some cars that I'd like to get rid of as time goes on. And I'd rather have another '33 three-window because I just enjoy them more. It's that 'forever thing,'" he smiles. "Chevelles aren't forever."

"I'll never finish all this stuff," Simard admits. "But that's OK. It's like somebody collecting stamps or other things that you can hold in your hand and look at. You derive pleasure out of them."

"Sometimes, when a car leaves, you have this real empty feeling, and you don't feel good for a long time," Simard admits. "From my experience, if I sold one of these cars I wouldn't be happy. Of course the money would be nice, but then you'd say, 'What am I going to do with the money? Am I going to buy something as interesting?' Probably not.'"

"I honestly look forward to coming out to the garage (it's right behind his house) every day. And it's just as much fun to work on other guys' cars as it is my own." "We're not seeing enough younger guys coming in," he notes, "but guys in it today are wanting vintage engines, like flatheads, hemis, Olds V-8s, and Caddys. They're recreating an era—the late '50s, early '60s—that's almost forgotten. Today's guys want to get stuff done sooner so they enjoy their cars. As for me," he smiles, "after 27 years of doing this full-time, it's still fun."

> " *You have to restore a car first, before making a hot rod out of it. If you don't you lose all the reference points. You need to maintain those reference points, or you constantly dig yourself a deeper hole.* "

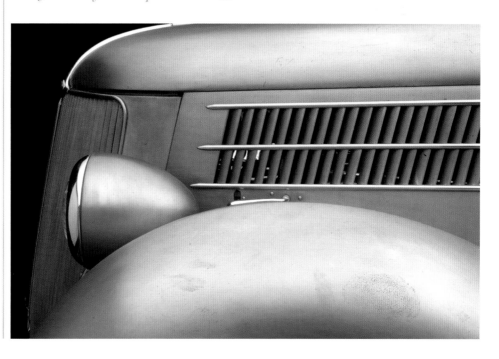

1932 FORD ROADSTER owned by Ken Gross

1932 FORD THREE-WINDOW COUPE owned by Mike O'Neill

1936 FORD *PHANTOM* TWO-DOOR PHAETON owned by Dave Nixon

1934 WILLYS *GASSER* COUPE owned by Steve O'Neill

In October 1992, at the Antique Automobile Club of America (AACA) Fall Meet in Hershey, Pennsylvania, dozens of enthusiastic spectators stood around a pair of freshly-restored 1932 Ford highboy hot rods, smiling and exchanging memories. Both cars were former California dry lakes racers, with authentic SCTA timing tags confirming their provenance. Kirk F. White, now of New Smyrna Beach, Florida, their owner, and the restorers, Jim Lowrey and his son, Jim Lowrey Jr., then of Tyngsboro, Massachusetts, watched proudly as both cars won coveted AACA Junior Awards. The roadsters returned in 1993 for Senior trophies. For Jim Lowrey Jr., who was already restoring antiques and classics, this was an important beginning. It indicated restoring historic hot rods could be a viable proposition. "I've

always fooled around with hot rods," Lowrey says. "My high school car was a '40 Ford coupe with a full-race flathead that my Dad built. In 1978, that was unheard of."

Lowrey's dad, a talented mechanic and machinist, owned a body shop for years, first doing conventional repair work, then edging into restoration. Racecars and hot rods were always part of the equation. Today, Jim Sr. is retired, but "he still builds all our flatheads. Nobody does *that* better."

Lowrey's shop, Lowrey Restorations in Tilton, New Hampshire, still turns out classic Packards, Cadillacs, and early Ford V-8 restorations, especially woodies. "But hot rod build-ups are the bulk of what we do. I still like doing the older cars," he adds. "Not

everyone wants a custom-built hot rod. But the tools and techniques we use for restoration work carry over into the traditional-style hot rods we build."

There's a recognizable Jim Lowrey approach when it comes to hot rods. His cars retain a traditional, almost stock-bodied look, but they're always smartly lowered, with great stances, steel wheels, and whitewalls. "We like our cars to look period-correct," Lowrey continues, "whether it's a '40s-era look, which I especially like, the earlier the better, or the '50s, '60s, or '70s. We'll use new crate motors, almost always Fords, if customers want them. Some people like the drivability of the new engines and suspensions.

"But there's still a call for the older engines. About half our cars have flatheads. My dad will build 'em from mild to wild. For most guys a 276-inch, not-really-radical flathead is just fine, but we'll fool with wilder camshafts, high compression, and more carburetors if a guy wants, and even build them over 300-cid. It all depends on what he's going to do with his car.

"I can't just *deliver* a vehicle," Lowrey explains. "I have to understand what a guy has in his mind. If he doesn't know exactly, we'll help coach him, but he has to feel that it's *his* decision. We know what we *like* to build, what we're best at doing. If someone suggests a radical, ultra-modern car, they can sense that I'm not into that. They either move more our way and are happy with that, or they realize we're just not the right shop to build that car.

"We've obviously developed our particular style. Our cars have an attitude of their own. I don't want to build an outrageous car. I like to keep our market somewhere in the middle. If you destroy all the original elements of an older car, it hurts its value. Ford did a tremendous styling job in the '30s. How do you re-invent a '32 Ford roadster?"

Plating aside, Lowrey and his crew do nearly everything in-house, with one exception. Petter Davidsen, up in Hampton Falls, New Hampshire, is Lowrey's upholsterer. "I'm trying to get him to move down here. He really understands my look," says Lowrey. "All my guys are happy working here. I've got a good crew now. Most of them came out of collision shops. They had the skills but weren't able to use their talent. Now, they're doing what they love. I've had to coach them to another level, but they consider this a dream job, compared to collision work. Sooner or later, I'll see applications from every good body man in the area.

"Right now I have seven people, and we've just added a new 5,000-square-foot assembly shop. I buy old cars whenever I can, like '32 three-window coupes and '34 roadsters. And I keep a variety of Brookville bodies. I'm always on the lookout for good cars. New Hampshire is picked pretty clean, but cars still turn up. Guys will call me and say they want, let's say, a '36 roadster, and I'll think, 'OK, who was I talking about who had one two years ago?' A lot of projects start like that.

"Now that I'm getting older, I'm having to bend the rules a little. But our new generation, the rat rod crowd, likes nice old-style cars, once they can afford them. Out of that group, a guy will pop up, kind of on the outer limits, and then he's a customer.

"We don't build cheap cars," he says thoughtfully. "But we're not the most expensive. Our cars are very high quality—they're for the guy who wants this look and can afford it. But it's like this: If a guy is a working man with a weekly paycheck, we can't build him a car."

"The selection of the top-75 '32 Fords of all time last year has really helped interest in our kind of car," Lowrey observes. "Now, younger guys want us to recreate that 'dry lakes' racing look. But not everybody wants a car out of 1940. Whether it's the '50s or the '70s, you have to be true to a theme." Lowrey grew up in these eras. He knows the differences cold.

And he really understands cars that were built long before he was born.

"Restoring the Ray Brown and Bob Schaenemann '32 roadsters was the best thing that ever happened to us," Lowrey says. "It started a lot of people doing those old cars. We didn't over-restore either one. Right from the beginning, we tried to do them the way they would have been done but really do them justice.

"I hadn't seen the Ray Brown car in years. Dad and I went to the 2007 Grand National Roadster Show, and it was there with the historic '32s. I really wanted to see how that Sherwood Green paint I did had held up. (Lowrey's specialty is painting, if you hadn't guessed.) It still looked great. Those two cars definitely set an industry benchmark. We tried to straddle the line between authenticity and over-restoration. Historic hot rods are getting hard to find today. We'd like to do as many as we can.

"Meanwhile, '39 and '40 Ford coupes are hot right now," says Lowrey, whose 75-years-young dad still drives one, along with the same '40 convertible he owned in high school. "You don't have to do a lot to them; they look great with just a few mild hot rod modifications."

> 66 *I can't just deliver a vehicle. I have to understand what a guy has in his mind.* 99

If you think there's a finite life to hot rod building, it's not evident up in rural New Hampshire. "I don't see any sign of a let-up," Lowrey says. "We sailed through the '80s, despite it being hard times for some companies. I have about 20 projects underway right now, and if we didn't get another order for a year, we'd still be fine. Of course, there's a lot of down time building these cars, looking for the right pieces, waiting for parts, for metal work, for machining, so it's a juggling act to keep everyone busy. My metal fabricator can whip a body together in no time. He keeps the body shop backed up." Seems to us, that's not a bad problem to have.

As this was written, Lowrey was heading for the Detroit Autorama to show a stunning '33 Ford roadster with a Weiand-blown flathead, owned by David Gazaway, that graced the May 2007 cover of *Street Rodder* magazine. "We've never shown one of our cars that far away," he says. "I like promoting our work, but I can't spend all my time doing that. I've got to be buckled down all the time."

He doesn't see himself ever competing for the coveted Ridler award. "I can't imagine spending that type of money on a car," he says. "We've never built a car that exceeded $200,000. In my eyes, our cars are just as nice, for a lot less money. I'm very proud of that."

Lowrey and his dad did a number of restorations a few years back for Ford collector Michael Dingman. The two were prominently mentioned in the RM Auction catalog when the Dingman Collection of Early V-8 Fords were sold, many for record prices, in Kensington, New Hampshire, in June 2006. "That got us a new customer from the Bay Area," says Lowrey, with evident pride. "He could have picked any number of shops on the West Coast, but he's sending all his cars to us."

"Although I don't want to be labeled a certain way, we're more like a production shop," Lowrey explains. "Work flows smoothly from one department to another. I realize you can't fondle something forever. You've got to finish what you do and move on to the next project. And all our cars are drivers. That's very important.

"This is my dream job, too. My dad had a very successful collision business, and when it came time to sell, he asked me if I wanted to continue it. I told him to take the money. I knew I could make this new business work with the right customers, hard work, and a little luck.

"Actually," he reflects, "you make your own luck."

1933 FORD ROADSTER
owned by David Gazaway

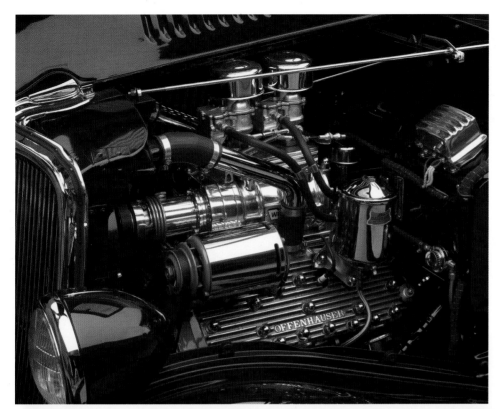

1932 FORD THREE-WINDOW COUPE
owned by Jim Lowrey Jr.

1935 FORD ROADSTER
owned by Michael Dingman

1932 FORD ROADSTER
owned by Jim Lowrey Sr.

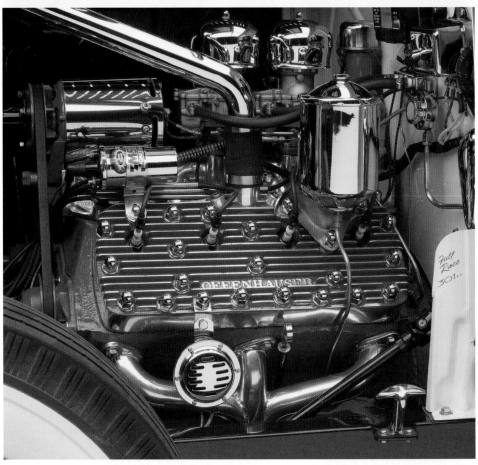

1934 FORD ROADSTER
owned by Jim Lowrey Jr.

CHAPTER 3

ROLLING BONES
These Guys Reinvented Attitude

At the National Street Rod Association's York, Pennsylvania, meet a few years back, I spotted two fenderless '32 Ford coupes parked side-by-side and about stopped in my tracks. Chopped unmercifully, clad in faded primer, with bare-bones interiors, they crouched next to one another like a pair of old alley cats, sunning themselves before another raid on the barrels. If my pal, Boston-based hot rod shooter Chuck Vranas had been there, I know just what he'd say. In the vernacular of the '50s, they were "wicked."

I sought out their owners, and although I didn't realize it at the time, these guys had begun a small revolution. Taking hot rodding to another extreme entirely, the dynamic duo of Ken Schmidt and Keith Cornell from the Albany, New York, area Rolling Bones Club (now proprietors of the Rolling Bones Hot Rod Shop), built a pair of cars that grabbed national attention and were featured in many magazines, despite their

unfinished look. As raw as you can get, they're mean-looking, noisy, and definitely in-your-face.

Schmidt's '32 3W ran a hot flathead. Cornell's power plant was a mid-'50s Ford Y-block. There was one disguised concession to modernity and cruising ease: they substituted Tremec 5-speeds with vintage-style shifters for the fragile old Ford boxes. Schmidt's coupe had a slightly-more-comfy-than-stock Ford front spring with Teflon buttons from POSIES. Unpainted, with bulldog front ends, straight '32 "fat" axles, original Guide 682-C headlights on chopped bars, louvered hoods and decks, sans mufflers, with bare metal interiors, minimal glass, and faded Mexican blankets for seat covers, both bad-boy three-windows were surrounded by ardent admirers who were convinced they had been built in Southern California back in the early '50s.

In fact, both cars were brand new, but they were constructed with authentic old parts. Their primered

surfaces had been artfully distressed to mimic the faded paint and dinged metal you'd expect from years of hard street and track life. Schmidt and Cornell drove their cars cross-country to California and stopped at Bonneville several times, adding to the coupes' virtually overnight legendry. On another occasion, the nasty New Yorkers appeared at the June L.A. Roadster Meet with a '32 Ford roadster that looked like the cool coupes' little brother. Think *Dennis the Menace* meets a '32 Ford.

The time-warped roadster was a real pantswetter with its faded and distressed black paint, a worn canvas top (stained with tea, I later learned, to look as through it were half a century old), a ratty-sounding flathead, and a faded leather interior, not to mention a genuine Southern California Timing Association dry lakes timing tag on the dash. Once again, Schmidt and Cornell really had heads nodding. "We're not interested in building cars with new or reproduction parts," Schmidt insisted. "Plenty of other guys do that."

"After I started my coupe, it took eighteen months. Keith had already started his frame, but after he saw what I was doing, he changed his plans and started again. My car is chopped five inches in front, four and three quarter inches in back. Keith did the chop."

At first, Cornell built a similar car, but he wanted one even lower. He found a clean stock-bodied 3W and wedge-chopped it 5 1/2 inches in front and 5 inches in the rear. "I didn't want a car with a filled roof," he says. "Both our coupes capture a style we loved from Don Montgomery's historic hot rod books. We've just copied all the great things those guys did in the past." Then they went a step further. Those radical chops, canted A-pillars, stretched wheelbases, and so-low stances make these cars look as though they are moving when they're standing still.

"We call 'em ten-percent cars,'" Schmidt says. "That means ten percent of the guys who see them would like them." But I've been there when the crowds gather, and I really think the 'thumbs-up' percentage is a lot higher.

"Our cars are aggressive, but approachable," Schmidt continues, warming to his subject. "They're not like $300,000-to-$400,000 show cars where there's no place for you to go with 'em. These cars make people smile; they want to hear them run and see them move. Right from the beginning, we wanted to use vintage engines like the flathead and the Y-block, but we've both got T-5 transmissions and we converted (from Ford torque tubes) to open drivelines. We built these cars to drive. We *wanted* to take them cross-country. We just had no idea people would go so nuts.

"When we drove to Bonneville, the response was such that we didn't know what to do. It was almost embarrassing. Of course we got 'salt fever.' Next, we planned to race that roadster. The flathead in it was one we borrowed for the trip cross-country. We took the windshield off, put on a tonneau cover and a roll cage, and tried to top 125 mph. I'm still trying to find some 18-inch Divco milk truck wheels for the rear. It's important to have the right look—and improve the rear end ratio, too."

Cornell says, "I started out as a Tri-year Chevy guy, but after hanging around with Ken and some of the older guys who were into '32 Fords, I realized how cool these cars were, and it rubbed off on me."

"That weathered appearance started with my coupe," says Schmidt. "I've had shiny cars you can polish all day long. Problem is, you have to keep cars like that clean; they don't look good dirty. That wasn't much fun. You look at the cars in those old books; those guys did it right. I like that feeling."

Schmidt and Cornell are taking orders for old-style cars with the down-and-dirty look they've obviously nailed. "We've got a stockpile of old front ends, axles, grilles, firewalls, and a few engine parts," says Schmidt. Their garage in Greenfield Center, New York, looks like a time warp, with parts piled high, ready to use. "We'll use Brookville bodies—they're awfully close to the real thing. Paint is an ongoing development. Other guys have tried to achieve that worn look. I'm not sure they know how to do it. I'm still learning, myself.

"With our roadster, I deliberately used an old windshield, chromed twenty-five years ago, and even put a small crack in it. The top was stained with tea. I tried to figure where it would be worn, discolored, and abused and then treated it accordingly. First, I covered everything with epoxy primer. Old Ford black paint has a blue cast to it. I can match that with flattener, add a few bubbles, even scratch the surface for the right patina where the normal wear would be, and the result is a car people feel very comfortable with—they don't have to be on guard or not touch it. These cars look great dirty. You can set your coffee down on one. And the look is evolving as we're getting better at it.

"We've enjoyed the attention our cars have gotten."

 We're not interested in building cars with new or reproduction parts. Plenty of other guys do that.

"One of the best things about these cars," adds Schmidt, "is that they are an instant ticket to meet and become friends with a lot of guys. In California, we stayed with people, some of them came East for Ty-Rods (the annual Ty-Rods Club meet each September), and went with us. I got the best compliment from one new friend who said, 'You guys build better old hot rods than we do in California.'"

"This whole thing has really been a trip," he says with a smile in his voice. "We're lookin' to build more cars. Really they're pieces of sculpture. We just have to find guys who like old hot rods the way we do, and want one of their own. But they have to remember, when you drive these cars six or seven hundred miles a day, you have to keep tools and parts in the trunk and be prepared to spend a half hour working on the car so you can drive it the next day."

"The guys who built these cars in the 1940s figured it all out," Schmidt says matter-of-factly. "My car has only one original idea and that's the rear license plate bracket. You have to have a sense of how a car should look. Most guys who build cars kind of bolt them together. They don't understand proportions. My '32 has a slightly extended wheelbase; it's still got the center door hinges; it doesn't have the gas tank hanging off the back that sorta slows things down. But you have to be careful not to get cartoony. It's easy to go too far visually."

Schmidt is an artist by profession. You can view his work at www.lonefeatherstudio.com. Cornell was an accident insurance claims adjuster. He's a crack wrench, besides. "We don't step on each other's toes artistically," Schmidt declares. They've subsequently built a pair of heavily hammered '32 Tudors for Dennis Varney, stuffed with a DeSoto hemi, and Mike Manno, running a SCoT-blown flathead. And they blew people away at the 2007 Grand National Roadster Show (GNRS) in Pomona with a track-nosed, Pierson Bros.-style '34 coupe for the street.

One image that sticks in my mind occurred a few years back at the annual Fathers' Day weekend L.A. Roadster Show. The two coupes and the roadster were parked in Mark Morton's *Hop Up* magazine corral for old-style cars. When they left to get a primo parking spot at the So-Cal Speed Shop open house, everybody stopped to look and listen. Unmuffled engines snarling, wheels kicking up dust, the trio in motion resembled a hot rod time warp, a snapshot taken when gow jobs prowled the streets and headed to the lakes on Friday nights. You'd have loved it.

1932 FORD ROADSTER owned by Ken Schmidt

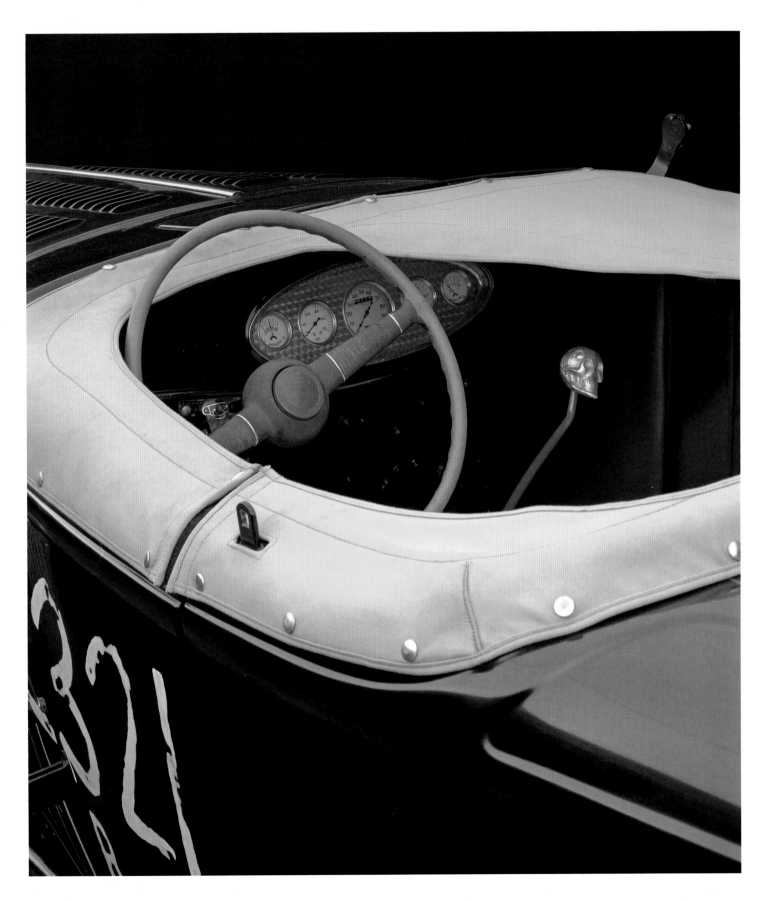

1932 FORD TUDOR owned by Mike Manno

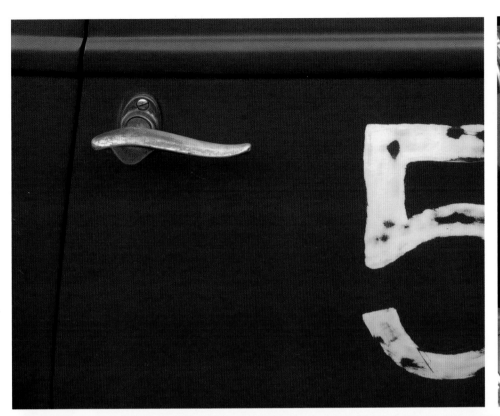

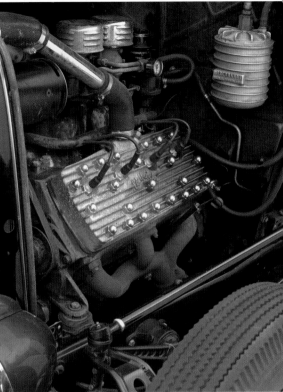

1932 FORD COUPE owned by Ken Schmidt

1932 FORD THREE-WINDOW COUPE
owned by Keith Cornell

CHAPTER 4

KEN "POSIES" FENICAL
Making a Statement

Ken Fenical, known as "POSIES" (his family owned a florist business), is one of the most creative, least conventional builders in the business. His shop in Hummelstown, Pennsylvania, just west of Hershey, turns out groundbreaking cars. Onlookers smile and nod. They scratch their heads in bewilderment and occasionally hate what they're seeing but grudgingly admit he's on to something.

After owning his first hot rod in 1959, he began building and pinstriping motorcycles. "Not knowing better," he says, using one of his favorite expressions, "I switched from bikes to cars, often working on projects someone else had started. I'd build it into a statement, where I was able to express myself through the car, then sell it."

"A statement," he explains, "is a car that's been reshaped in a way that nobody else has done before. I might think of an idea, and when I finally do it, I might end up seeing it on some vintage car from the '30s. So I can't take all the credit. Let's call it an influence, whether it's subliminal or not. Like my doing a hardtop on a '32 roadster, or putting a spare tire in the fender well. When I did that, nobody in the U.S. used it in the magazines, but the Europeans liked it, and I developed a following over there."

"I still strive for individual cars that are statement-makers," POSIES says. "I look at what's there, then I enhance it, in a hot rod way.

"After realizing other people wanted to own my finished cars more than I did, I started targeting that aspect. I wanted to show potential customers that I had the ability to make their projects excel. Alternatively, I could offer my thoughts to their thoughts to make a car outstanding."

Back in 1981, the irrepressible Fenical built a yellow '36 Ford with a Carson-style padded top. "People had forgotten what the past was about. This cool custom reminded them. My touch was the LaSalle grille shell, but I flipped it upside-down so it mated perfectly with the hood line. And I lowered the spare instead of removing it. This car may have been one of the first old-style customs that was nose-diving instead of tail-dragging." As a hot rodder, he says, "I didn't appreciate tail-draggers, and I still don't."

POSIES has a keen designer's eye, a metal wizard's delight in reshaping steel, a mechanic's dexterity, and an inventor's curiosity. There isn't anything he won't attempt if he feels it will result in an exceptional car. Working in a small Pennsylvania town, he's long understood the importance of garnering national attention.

"I didn't know the magazine industry was as close as it really is," he confesses. "It's out there for the taking. The publicity opened another kind of world to me. The late Gray Baskerville was a big influence on my '36. That car was featured in 28 worldwide publications, a phenomenal feat at that time. It struck a responsive chord. *That's* an example of making a statement."

"In '87, after (the late) L'il John Buttera brought the monochromatic look to the surface, I mixed it up a little. I wasn't ready for full color," he notes modestly. "So I separated colors vertically on my '38 Ford convertible sedan. The front was red; the rear was black, and I painted the billet wheels. Three months later, (the late) Boyd Coddington painted a set of billet wheels yellow. It's great when the things we do become strong editorially, or they're photogenic, but that's just the start. "If you can take a flip-down license plate and make a kit out of it, like Dan Fink, then make money selling it, *that* funds your drive for more projects."

POSIES' big moneymaker was his Super Slide Spring. "I realized that [the late] Jim Ewing made a tube axle that was never standard. In 1968, I told Ewing, Pete Chapouris, and Jim Jacobs, 'You need to make a standardized tube axle that fits fendered cars.' Every time I ordered one of their axles, it was an eighth-inch or quarter-inch different. I said, if you standardize it, I'll provide a spring for it. Later, when they did I-beam axles, I could standardize the spring, provide different heights [stock, reverse-eye, and super-low], and assign part numbers." Today, POSIES builds and sells many different springs, along with other suspension parts.

"Could we sell this? Should we sell this? That's always our thought," he says. "We're only here because of our drive, and our stick-to-itiveness."

To POSIES, the creative process is a constant turn on. You can see it in a long line of imaginative rides that resemble nothing else: the *Flathead Flyer*, *Phunkie '32*, *Extremeliner*, *Aeroliner*, and his latest ride, the *Fleetliner*, are all polarizing cars. With every POSIES statement, visual excitement spikes up another notch. "What would *this* be like?" he speculates, then he builds it. "That's part of not knowing better," he jokes. "If I did, I'd be doing something more important."

POSIES has a set of rules for would-be clients. "We like them to go to three or four national meets, ask questions, go on a learning curve, even visit two or three other shops before they become our customers. Most importantly, we want them to find a car that meets their standards."

"I need to find out what a customer wants," he continues. "If he's married, what are his wife's likes and desires? Does he understand colors? How involved is she? When I understand what he wants to build, I get them to pull colors out, once I hear what they're creating, then challenge them. I ask, 'What if this would be better?' When they buck me, I get back to where they want to be, or take it to a second challenge to make sure it's correct. And I re-guide them if necessary.

"Seldom do I ever get to build a car from scratch, *my way*, for someone else. But I've been fortunate to do cars that were strong statements for other people—like that '57 Chevy for Vic Edelbrock, Jr., the Nash Metro for Steve Irbie of Kicker Stereo, and Bill Kolovani's '41 Willys.

"It's too easy to blend into the background, to disappear," POSIES insists. "That's what it's all about; you want to be an individual, so you go for it. I just do what satisfies me, for the moment. Each of my projects is a fun statement, and they're all individualistic.

"When I pulled the cover off to reveal the Aeroliner at the SEMA (Specialty Equipment Market Association) Show, a lot of people were there. It's a nice experience, but you can't pay bills with it; you can't eat it. I appreciate the glory, but the big thing is being able to accomplish the project and make the statement. Once that's been done, I look forward to the experiences that come from it: the chance to exhibit at the Petersen Museum, to meet Jay Leno on Rodeo Drive, to go to Meadow Brook, to become friends with Jack Roush, to talk to BF Goodrich about a tire design—*that's* the best."

Asked which car he's most proud of, he says, unhesitatingly, "My red and black '38 Ford—10-point roll cage, Henry Hi-Rise tailpipes, like sitting in a Cadillac, 427 side oiler, like a big-block '32, only it's a four-passenger hot rod. *That's* the one I'd like to own back.

"Most fun in a car? That'd be my '32 Phunkie. The day I finished it, I drove it cross-country, participated in the *Hot Rod* Power Tour, got up in the morning in Santa Fe, with snow all over the car, turned on the heater and went down the road. It was the first Brookville roadster body sold. My first attempt at a '32 was not like anybody else's. I called it Phunkie so they couldn't criticize the funkiness."

His proudest moment? "Dave McClellan was the speaker at the 1999 Detroit Autorama, in front of the Big Three. 'I'd like to introduce you to POSIES, with the Extremeliner,' he said. 'That's where the PT Cruiser came from.' Tears came to my eyes because we always thought that.

"I think we should pat the rat rodders on the back," he concludes. "They're building crude, rude, hard machines. Keith Weesner said it best: 'They're just not finished.' I'd be at a nice-sized car meet and I'd see affluent couples with a hundred thousand dollars in their cars, going toward a rat rod, just fascinated. There was *something* there.

"I'm not into the ratty aspect. I like the creativity and ingenuity, but I like my cars to be finished and safe to drive. So I built the '29 ThunderRoad pickup, owned by Scott Whitaker of Dynamat, into what I used to see coming out of California. Josh Shaw, a renowned faux painter, paid me a big compliment. He was leaning against a building, looking at that truck's profile for an hour, studying. He's just a young guy, and he approved of the things I did. You've got to love that."

1937 STUDEBAKER
EXTREMELINER
owned by John O'Quinn

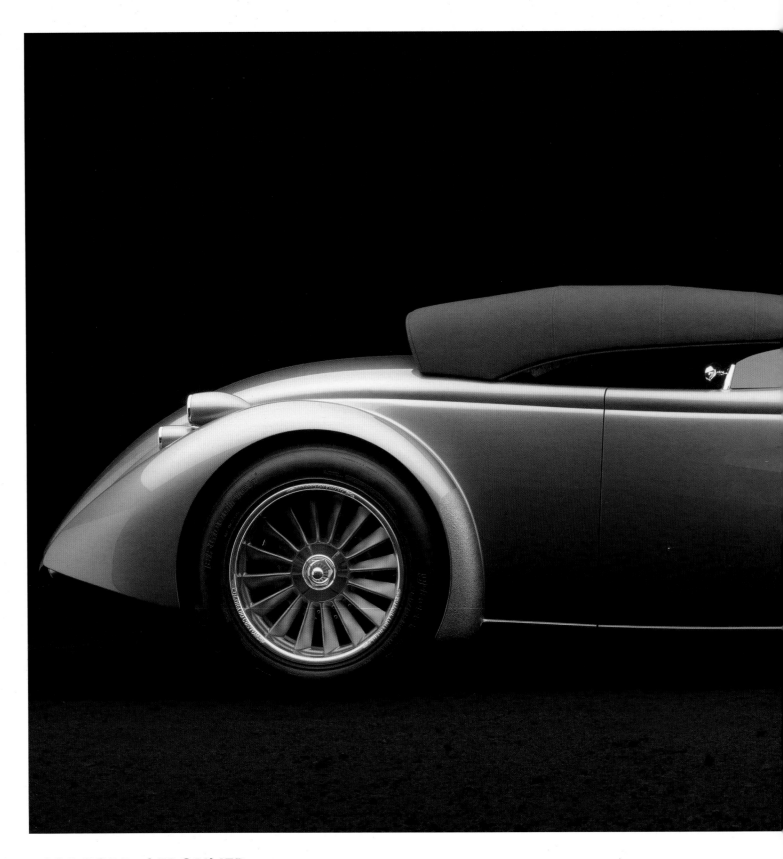

1935 FORD *AEROLINER* owned by Richard Ullman

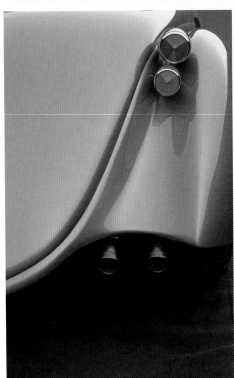

1941 WILLYS *GASSER* COUPE owned by Bill Kolovani

CHAPTER 5

ALAN JOHNSON
They'll Stop at Nothing

At the SEMA show a few years ago, I stopped in my tracks when I spotted Alan Johnson's '37 Ford three-window coupe, an all-steel car that resembled a small Lincoln-Zephyr. Although the Briggs Manufacturing Company designed a full-sized '37 clay model, Ford Motor Company never did a production three-window. Johnson never saw that prototype's photo, but he'd outdone the Briggs designers anyway, with a much prettier roofline. "Chip Foose helped," said Johnson. "I'd asked him to do some dash renderings and told him I was having a problem with the roof. Ten minutes later, he sent me a sketch with a different radius. Nobody's hit a '37 like that."

Johnson's Hot Rod Shop in Gadsden, Alabama, may be off the beaten track, but there's not much these guys haven't tried and very little they can't do. Nothing scares them, from traditional hot rods to modernized muscle, phantom woodies and Super Rod trucks to a sleek, record-setting, contemporary Bonneville car. "My interests are varied," Johnson says, "like my customers'. If a project excites me and my guys, we'll go at it 110 percent. It's just got to turn me on."

Take the sleek Cadillac XLR that his shop did for Bonneville last year. It was Johnson's first salt flats effort, and without testing or tuning—with Gramie Bartles driving—it hit a record 222 mph. "I always wanted to do a Bonneville car," Johnson says, "but we had a lot of help with the chassis setup and pre-tech. I like to do as much as possible in-house, but I'm smart enough to call somebody when I'm over my head."

"I really don't like doing the same thing over and over. While I like the traditional look, with most of my customers I'm able to make some changes and modern improvements. The only things we don't do in-house are engines, plating, and upholstery. I kind of wish we did engines because it seems we're always having to do some engine work, especially if it's an unusual one."

Johnson seems to have struck a perfect balance between old and new, accentuating each car's special attributes with subtle changes. "That black '32 three-window is a car I started for myself six years ago, then sold to a customer. With it, we're trying to mix the older style with some modern touches. I hope the traditionalists still like it. That coupe was a nice car to begin with . . . I tell my customers: Start with the best piece you can. In the long run, when you're talking about metal work, it's much more affordable."

"Good old stuff still turns up out here," says Johnson, who's always on the lookout for future project material. "I've found more '32 Fords in the last three years. I uncovered a '32 sedan, just two miles from the shop, that's been sitting for thirty years. I'd known about it for some time, but they weren't ready to sell." He doesn't have to redo every car he finds. "It's just an old hot rod, so I'll leave it pretty much the way it is, with an old repaint in lacquer."

Although the older cars aren't in demand for some builders, that's not the case down in Alabama. "The biggest majority of our work right now is '32 Fords," he continues. "I've got five cars in process and eight more waiting to start. We have a lot of repeat customers, and they like different kinds of cars. We recently did a '55 Chevy for that '32's owner. We started with an original 24,000-mile car, but now it's got a new driveline and a 700-horsepower big-block. He just wants to enjoy it and drive it."

"We try to build everything we do as a driver," Johnson adds, "even if we know it's not going to be driven. But really, if it's not a driver, it's not much good to us. Vernon Walker, from the NSRA, has a '32 Ford we did that nobody's ever seen in a magazine. He drives it to work, parks it in his lot, and takes it to all his shows. It's been at SEMA in the NSRA booth. After four years, it's got 103,000 miles now," Johnson says, obviously pleased that Walker's car is extensively used."

Johnson's Hot Rod Shop received considerable acclaim from a radical newer car called the *G-Force Cuda.* The idea was to take an historic muscle car—in this case a chopped and sectioned '71 Barracuda—and transform it into an ultra-high-performance street machine. Under the reshaped carbon fiber hood was a dry-sump, 572-cid, 870-bhp, Indy cylinder head all-aluminum hemi. The car also had an Art Morrison chassis, a roll cage, carbon fiber front fenders and doors and other components to keep weight down to 2,800 pounds, Corvette C5 suspension all around, with the Corvette's Getrag transaxle, six-piston front brakes, and a long list of top-notch components from the best suppliers. The goal was a 200-mph missile.

"We did this car for a very good customer, Bob Johnson," Alan notes. "Earlier, we'd done a Camaro project with a Donovan V-8 and a six-speed for Bob that made the cover of *Popular Hot Rodding,* and he ran that car on the *Hot Rod* Power Tour. That led to this bright orange 'Cuda, which came out before Dodge showed its new Challenger. We never got to run it at Maxton, but the guys from Dodge had a good look at it, and they approved. We'd never fooled with something that complex before, so it was a learning experience."

Bob Johnson is a dream customer for Johnson's Hot Rod Shop. His projects have included a 1947 Ford Phantom two-door woodie and a '56 Ford F-100 with a Triton V-10 engine. "We did all the woodwork on that wagon." Alan says. We'd never done wood before. When we told some wood guys what we needed, they didn't want to do it. Once we started, we understood why. Every piece of wood on that car has a radius that flows off the steel panels. With a stock woodie, you get to use the old wood as a pattern. Here, we had to do the first curved edge, then create the rest, all by hand." Alan and Tony Inman made polyurethane foam patterns to help them visualize the wood pieces. The wagon was topped with a canvas-covered one-piece aluminum roof. We're talking concept-car complexity here.

The woodie's intricacies extended to a 4-valve, 4-cam, 4.6-liter Cobra engine. "Ford Performance put me onto a guy who was supposed to know everything about that engine," says Johnson. "When it was clear that he couldn't help, we just engineered it ourselves." Johnson's shop fabricated a new upper intake manifold, in order to relocate the throttle body to the front of the engine, then they topped it off with a free-flowing fiberglass intake plenum. The dash, a modern update of the original shape, was first formed in foam and then finished in fiberglass. The car debuted at the SEMA show where it was a hit. I remember thinking, "Alabama be damned, Johnson's had to be some shop to accomplish this level of craftsmanship."

> **❝** *I tell my customers: Start with the best piece you can. In the long run, when you're talking about metal work, it's much more affordable.* **❞**

Alan will show sketches to some customers. Other times he'll do a car without artwork. "It kind of depends on the car," he says. "We like it when customers give us free rein, but sometimes you have to show a guy what you're doing. Over the last five years, the majority of our business is from repeat customers. I like that because you know what to expect from them, and they know what to expect from you. Many of them have become really close friends."

Although he's often used the SEMA show as a launch pad for his finished cars, "I'm really not a big fan of indoor shows," he insists. "When you look at the winners these days, it looks like some promoters aren't doing a good job. Reflecting on the AMBR results a few years back, Johnson commented, "I thought the So-Cal/Jimmy Shine Ardun '32 had it sewn up. The winner was a '36 Ford that was a very different car. I don't know exactly how the judging was done. I think the winning car should be really beautiful. Nothing else matters. When it's all about whether each of the bolts are in synch with each other, the award loses credibility. It'd be a nice feather in our cap to win the Ridler [one of his cars was a runner-up a few years back], but it's hard nowadays. You have to have the right customer. There are no guarantees. And guys like Chip [Foose] and Troy [Trepanier] keep raising the bar."

Johnson's current effort on a beautifully re-proportioned '32 Ford Model B400 epitomizes his philosophy of subtly blending old and new elements. "I want to keep what Henry had," he explains, "but with the feeling of something like a classic Duesenberg. The body proportions are now more like those on a Vicky. The bumpers have been thinned out. We've changed the look and the diameter of the wheels as well as the rear tire size, and now we're using Dayton wires. I think wheels and tires have to grab your attention. If they do, *then* you'll walk over to look more closely at a car. You won't walk over to a car just for slick paint, if it doesn't have the stance to start with."

"This business is still exciting for me," Johnson says. "It's fun to come to work each day, seeing the cars we're doing, and getting out the work. I don't have the money to have a car collection, but we do so many different things here, it doesn't matter. I just can't image doing a regular job."

1933 FORD CABRIOLET owned by Doug Cooper

1932 FORD FIVE-WINDOW COUPE owned by Bill Roberts

1932 FORD
THREE-WINDOW COUPE
owned by Ron Winter

1932 FORD B400
owned by Doug Cooper

1947 FORD *PHANTOM WOODIE* TWO-DOOR
owned by Bob Johnson

1937 FORD WOODIE
owned by Wesley Johnson

Modest, taciturn, right to the point, with a Southern drawl that reflects his Tennessee origins, Bobby Alloway's got a sharp perspective on hot rods. His cars have an unmistakable look, whether it's a Deuce roadster, a '34 Ford coupe, a '56 Ford Crown Vic, or a '57 T-Bird.

Although he'd done a few International Show Car Association (ISCA) shows back in 1985, his Louisville, Tennessee, shop came out of nowhere when he won the coveted Detroit Autorama Ridler Award with an ultra-smooth, bright red '33 Ford Victoria, built on his own time with his own money. "We *needed* to win," he later reflected. "We needed the money to get back home."

Bobby credits his two '33 Ford "flame cars," a coupe and a roadster, in 1995–96, for his big break. "Before that, about 90 percent of flame jobs were on primered cars," he recalls, "usually done to cover-up something. Nobody had ever done two at once." These cars were jet black (his favorite color), absolutely on fire, and they really stood out from the crowd.

People took notice. And Bobby Alloway was off and running.

His early coupes and roadsters follow a pattern that never gets old. In his words, "They've got big 'uns and little 'uns, and an over-the-top rake." I'd add that they're radically lowered, with four-bars nearly on the pavement, big and little ETIII wheels ("They just *have* to be on a hot rod," he says, "and Boyd's [Coddington] front wheels are a pretty good match."), full fenders, and they may be fabulously flamed.

Alloway's favorite form of motivation is a big-block 500-plus-cid Chevy rat motor that's been carbed, cammed, and chromed to the hilt, but he's segued into SOHC 427 Ford 'cammer motors. Either way, they're real hot rods. "In this shop," Alloway explains, "we build our cars around the tires and wheels. That's where some guys screw up. They do the car and *then* add the wheels. We *start* with 'em."

On his early cars there are always just enough original Ford pieces, like oversized Commercial headlights (with directional signals inside), chopped taillight stands and gennie grilles—artfully mixed with chopped tops, subtle body modifications that accentuate a '30s-era Ford's already clean proportions, and classic architecture. "There's no need for bumpers," he says. "The gas filler is hidden, and the rear pan is trimmed to match the bobbed fenders. It's just cleaner that way."

His artful sculpting takes already beautiful bodies, then tweaks them just so. What remains is the essence of the pure Ford- or Chevy-inspired original shape that's been tantalizing hot rodders for decades. "That's why we can build a '57 T-Bird and it still looks like one of our cars. On that 'Bird, we stretched the wheelbase seven inches and gave the front fenders a little more proportion. I don't want to take a really pretty car and jack with it," he says modestly. "But if you get the stance, the tires, and the wheels right, everybody will like it."

"We're finishing up a Ford Starliner right now with a 'cammer motor," he notes. "It's got custom aluminum valve covers and an air cleaner for the two 4-bbls that resembles a factory Ford part, but it's twice as wide. We're doing a '64 Galaxie XL interior for it, with all the chrome trim on the seats. I like working with what the manufacturers did. Why would you change something that's beautiful?"

Alloway's cars are very, very low, just short of cartoon-like in their forms. He says his biggest influence was Thom Taylor. "He was always drawing coupes with their front fenders practically on the ground. In his sketches, in profile, the lower curve of the front fender radius really hangs down over the front tires. I'd seen Tom's pictures, liked the look, and tried for years to get my cars that low."

You simply can't get that low with just a dropped axle and reversed spring eyes. On an early car, Alloway starts with a pair of boxed side rails, then he adds his own tubular cross-members and a five-inch tubular dropped axle. The grille is laid back about an inch and a half at the top and pulled out one inch at the bottom. That trick picks up the front fenders about an inch and a half. The hood and the sides have been shortened slightly to fit. That modification keeps everything very low, with the fenders perfectly positioned over the wheel centers and the "V" grille point still above ground.

By the way, Bobby's often used chopped fiberglass bodies by Rat's Glass, but his fenders are repro steel items from Funk in Ohio. "It's the reverse of the way a lot of people do it," he explains. "Fiberglass requires a lot less work than a metal body; the metal ones are getting hard to come by, and most of 'em have six inches of mud on 'em, anyway. And steel fenders fit so much better than glass ones. It's simple. If I were building a car to keep for years, it's got to be steel. But if I'm doing one to just get out in and enjoy, it can be glass. Fiberglass doesn't scare me."

Here's a trade secret: Although they're way down in the weeds, Alloway's early cars are eminently drivable, thanks to custom deep-drop front cross-members and spacer blocks that incorporate soft rubber snubbers that can be altered to raise or lower the car's height. The front frame horns are bobbed, and the frame is C-notched above the front (and rear) axles for adequate spring perch clearance. That gives his cars about two inches of suspension travel.

Anchored by Viper shocks and capped by Pete & Jake's spring shackles and a plated, flattened, POSIES transverse spring with reversed eyes, the front axle will move about an inch vertically before it cushions against the snubbers. Alloway insists you never feel it when it hits. "You don't get 'em any lower and still drive 'em. The frame rails are notched where the rear fender meets the frame, and the rear axle is narrowed on each side, so those big

> 66 *I like working with what the original manufacturers did. Why would you change something that's beautiful?* 99

275/70 x 16 rear tires fit neatly in the confines of the bobbed fenders.

Why the passion for big-blocks? Says Alloway, "You can build up a small-block, spend a bunch of money, and a stock big-block will run just as good. Big-blocks have an undeserved bad reputation. They're not a high rpm motor. They're torquey. But we're not racing. We're just running from red light to red light. That's when you want a stout motor, and that's what these engines are. And they don't cost a lot of money."

"People *think* they'll have fit problems," he continues, "but they're only a bit wider than small-blocks—two inches by two inches by two inches. You do need twenty-three to twenty-four inches of frame width. We run the A/C and accessories on the bottom for a cleaner look and better clearance. You also need a 'Vette or Chevy truck pan." He's experimented with several cams to find the right combination. "Before I'll do something for someone else," he says, "I'll do it on my own car first."

Although he won the Ridler years ago, he's realistic about competing today. "It's become as much about the presentation and the build book now as it is the car," he notes, almost wistfully. "I think they've forgotten the original purpose of the award, and instead, it's like a Hollywood production. It's supposed to be about a craftsman or a shop building a great car. But all that's changed. I can't ask a customer to spend $2 to $3 million, just for bragging rights.

"I've got a '37 Chevy coupe I'm building, with a lot of modifications. And people have told me I ought to take it to Detroit. It sounds real good, but you look at the cars that are winning now, and it's a reality check, really a gut check. You can't beat unlimited money and talent, when a customer is willing to spend whatever it takes. You can *see* the money. So I've bowed out."

"On the other hand," Alloway notes with satisfaction, "my customer's car will be really nice, and he can *drive* his car when we're through."

As a kid, Alloway cut his teeth on '55, '56, and '57 Chevys, buying cars, fixing them up, selling them, and starting over again. "But we're all getting older," he notes. "I drove those Chevys, but I *wanted* a '32 or a '33 Ford. Now, the younger guys want those 'tri-year' Chevys. They're not into the older cars as much. We're building that 'cammer '61 Starliner that looks really retro, as if it could have been done back in the day. We're also doing a '55 Buick convertible and a '61 Chevy 'bubbletop.' I like that we can build a car like that '57 Thunderbird for SEMA, and people know immediately, it's *our* car. Although we've got a couple of them going, the older cars, the early street rods, are kind of dead right now. But they'll come back. They always do."

Alloway has high-profile clients, including George Poteet, George Lange, and Tom Clark, but he works with many other guys who aren't as well-known. "It doesn't matter," he says. "They both deserve and they both get the same effort. The only difference is that with a wealthier client, if you need to buy or make a part that you think would really help the car, you can do it. With other guys, you might have to work a little harder for the same effect. But really, it's not about the money. We do our best for everybody."

"It's really hard to get on top," he notes. "And even harder to stay there. There are a lot of talented young kids today with great ideas. While I'd like to stay with the older cars, you have to go where the trend is going to stay competitive. Actually, you have to go there first."

1932 FORD ROADSTER owned by Bobby Alloway

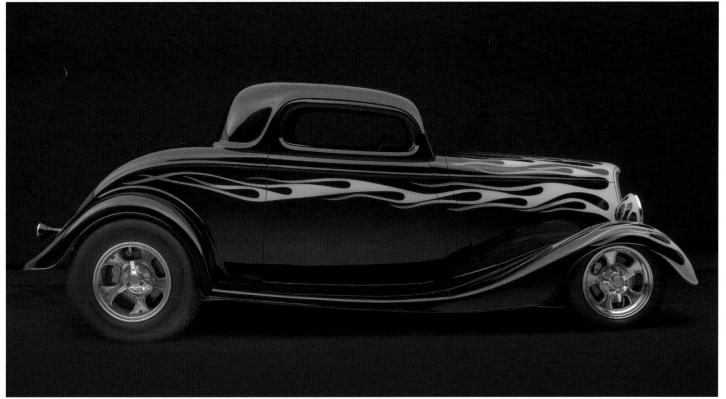

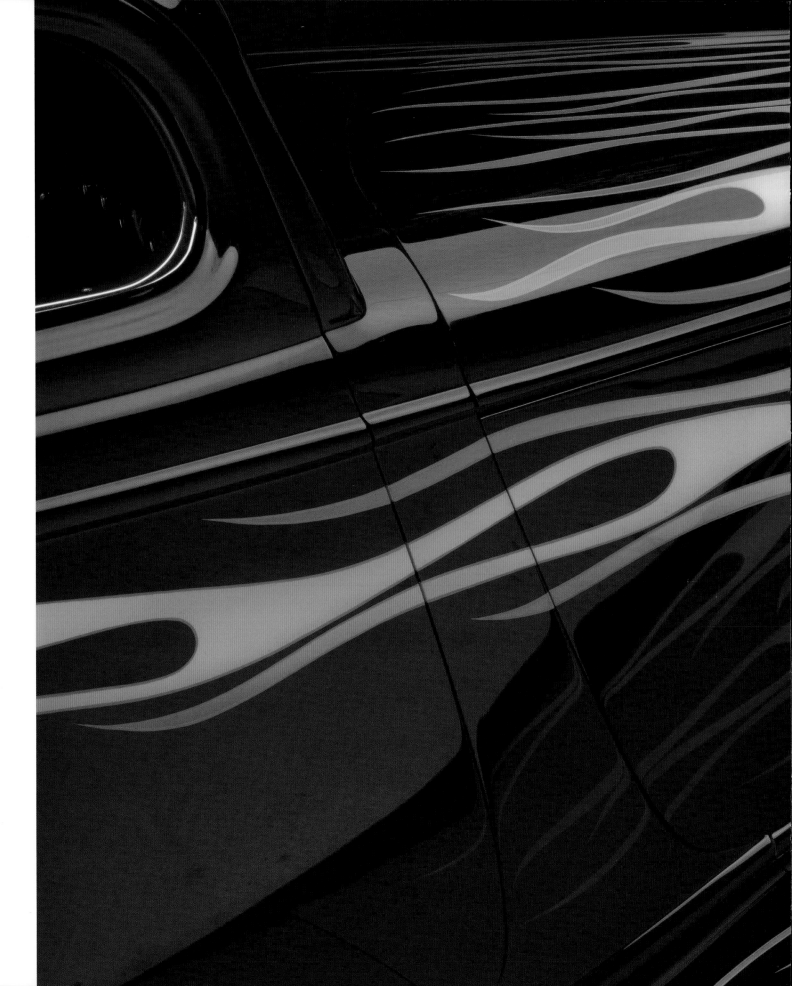

1937 CHEVROLET
FIVE-WINDOW COUPE
owned by Chuck and Diane Rowe

1949 FORD CONVERTIBLE
owned by Bobby Alloway

CHAPTER 7

TROY TREPANIER
Boy Genius

When he was 16, Troy Trepanier of Manteno, Illinois, seriously hot-rodded his grandfather's Chevelle. After cutting his teeth in his dad's shop for four years, he opened Rad Rides by Troy. Out came the *Sniper*, a dark green, Viper-powered, "new age" '54 Plymouth built for rodding's genial patron, George Poteet. This seminal effort put Trepanier squarely on the map, virtually overnight. The Sniper epitomized his philosophy. An unusual model choice, it was beautifully built, finished in an uncommon hue, with an edgy-for-the-time Viper powertrain, and it could be (and was) confidently driven cross-country.

"When I started doing cars," Trepanier explains, "I didn't have a lot of money. And I thought a lot of popular cars looked the same. I wanted to make a statement. When you do an unusual car, and you do it tastefully, like that Plymouth, or our '50 Buick, or the Rambler station wagon, people can't really compare it to anything. You don't have to stretch it out; it's already got a different look, so it can stand on its own. You're 50 percent ahead of the game, and you don't have to change as much. I try to do that with every car."

Trepanier's not an Art Center School graduate, nor is he an engineer, but you could stack him up against any of those professionals, and he'd match them, skill for skill, theory for theory. His cars are often finished in unusual shades, most frequently, variations on a green theme. "With colors," he explains, "I like to be different, so as to really create something out of the ordinary. If we'd done the Sniper in black, it wouldn't have been half as appealing. We do a lot of two-tone treatments. Using colors that way lets you control the shape of the body. You can make it appear thinner. Most interiors nowadays are variations on blacks, browns, and grays. We've got much more freedom. Our external colors let us do some beautifully contrasting interiors.

"With our '62 Chevelle, a car called *Chicane*, we used a muddy Army green. The customer's first comment to me was, 'Are you whacked?' But he agreed with me we'd nailed it once he saw it. We're fortunate. Because we're known for our colors, most customers will let us pick them. They know why they're here. But I won't do a spray-out too early because you can pick a color too soon and people change their minds. I'll ask a customer to give me a tone and we'll go from there. Look, it's *their* car; they've got to be on board at least 95 percent. Then, we'll work together. Ross Myers kept sending me color samples; he even sent a Tiffany box. Then I showed him that Cordova tan, and he liked it. He later said, 'I kept sending Troy my ideas but he went his own way.'

"Now, to be honest," he admits, "we are doing a purple and silver Corvette. I lost that battle. But the colors fit *that* type of car."

Trepanier defines success as "having the right customers, and having good rapport and friendship with them. Plus," he emphasizes, "we have a *terrific* team of guys. Customers like George Poteet give you the support you need to get the job done right. My grandpa always said, 'There's only one way to do things and that's the right way.' I live by that rule."

Part of Trepanier 's impressive 2007 success involved winning the Detroit Autorama's coveted Ridler Award the first time he tried, with a radical chopped, channeled, and sectioned '36 Ford coupe for Ross and Beth Myers called *First Love*. "Sometimes you *know* you have the right customer when you hear about the car," says Trepanier. "Ross told me he got that '36 when he was just nine years old. And then he kept it all those years. The story was more exciting to me than the car. He had a dream and we helped him realize it."

For a guy who likes working on newer models, in Trepanier's words, "that car was a challenge. There's only so much you can do to the top, and it still looks like an old car. And we started with an original car; we didn't make it up. So we worked hard underneath, on the suspension, on all the finishes; and it became another car entirely. We had a clean sheet of paper. You simply cannot compare the result to any other '36 Ford.

"I've said that I have no intention of competing for the Ridler again. It was very enjoyable because we have a really tight group. And I wanted to show what we were capable of doing at this point in time. I got very excited about this project. But we didn't just go there to win the Ridler. Plenty of people have already done that. Chip raised the bar with the *Impression* '36 Ford roadster for Ken Reister. We went there to raise it further.

"Beth Myers, Ross's wife, had the best compliment about the '36. She said, 'It looks like a beautiful piece of jewelry.'"

Creativity is a continuous process for Trepanier and his team. "A lot of it is done on the run," he admits. "And it can be having a beer after work, in the shop, just thinking and talking. It's a group effort. One of my theories, and I say it all the time, is that things don't have to look heavy. I tell my guys we're here to create. We don't hurry the process, but we're pretty efficient. We do look at everything very closely. We do all our panels with a step line in mind, with an eye for two-tone paint. I want things to be flowing, symmetrical, clean and simple. So thinking that way becomes a habit."

He's fond of talking about giving parts and pieces an "OEM appearance," loosely translated (in Troyspeak) as the way an original equipment manufacturer would create an important part or a panel. "We strive to make all our parts look that way. Chip [Foose] gets this too," he continues. "With the *Grand Master*, the '35 Chevy two-door sedan he did for Wes Rydell, Chip achieved a factory

'concept car' look. A car doesn't have to make an outrageous statement. It can be a statement in its own simplicity, its own perfection."

For Trepanier, the devil is definitely in the details. "Every car has a distributor cap," he notes, "so why does it have to stand out when you can blend it in and make it go away? There's very little plating that shines on our cars; we use nickel and satin finishes to make suspension parts like A-arms appear even more slender. With all our chassis now, we carefully finish and smooth small sections and blend them together to achieve a hydro-formed look. We take .090 chromoly steel, run it through a Pullmax machine so when it's finished it appears like a stamping or a casting, but very high-end."

> ❝ *When you do an unusual car, and you do it tastefully, people can't really compare it to anything. You don't have to stretch it out; it's already got a different look, so it can stand on its own.* ❞

Stemming from the Viper engine years ago in Poteet's Plymouth, all Trepanier's cars have impressive engines. "We're building cars with Nextel Cup V-8s, with Mercedes-Benz V-8s. We're doing a '69 Torino for George with a Boss 429. We do cars with LS-1 injected Chevys," he says. "We used to do our own assembly, in house, but now I've got the best engine guy and he's just 25 miles away. He did our Bonneville motor. We do all the de-burring and slicking-up of blocks and components, he machines and assembles the internals, then we do final work here and test them on our own chassis dyno.

"Modern electronic fuel injection lets you hide a lot of things," he confides. "It's endless, the sort of stuff we can do, like on a '70 Nova we're building with a 572 big-block that's got a lot of '69 Camaro influence, we've mounted a ProCharger (supercharger) backwards, with a separate EFI

unit, located out of sight, in the fender. Best of all, it runs like a watch.

"That's my big thing—mechanical fabrication, chassis work, and plumbing. And it's what we're known for. I take a lot of pride in that. Eaton is one of our sponsors. They own Aeroquip, so we have every possible choice of lines and fittings, right here in the shop. I like making things look like something they're not. We're very good at that."

Asked if he uses any renderings, concept sketches, etc., as a guide to construction, "Zero" is the answer. "Although, to be honest, we do *some* visualizing. Bob Thrash does it for me, and I have a couple of talented kids in the shop who can draw. I was a mechanic before I became a fabricator, so I believe something has to work well before it can be made to look good. That's made a big difference in what we do—and it makes everything better."

Function is very important to Trepanier. "I really like when people look at our cars and just want to get in 'em and torture 'em. Although we build the best hand-crafted cars, I'm not much for restoring things. I want people to *want* to drive our cars. We spend time making them work so they can."

Rad Rides built a killer Bonneville Barracuda with a turbocharged 4-cylinder engine for George Poteet they called *Blowfish*, and it set a record well over 200 mph right out of the box. Trepanier plans to install a Nextel Dodge R5 ethanol-powered V-8 and up the record to 300 mph. He'd like to build a Baha off-road racer, and he's talking with Ross Myers about building "the World's Fastest Mustang," another salt flats stormer. Meanwhile, he's got a '56 Chrysler 300 underway ("I've always liked those cars"). He did an extraordinary '40 Ford convertible, with a disappearing top, for the SEMA show that's arguably the most contemporary effort ever made on one of Henry's finest models, and he's thinking ahead. "We've never had a car on the lawn at Pebble Beach," he muses.

1969 CHEVROLET CAMARO TWO-DOOR HARDTOP owned by Mark Ruane

1962 LINCOLN FOUR-DOOR CONVERTIBLE owned by Manny Ramirez

1932 FORD ROADSTER owned by Roger Ritzow

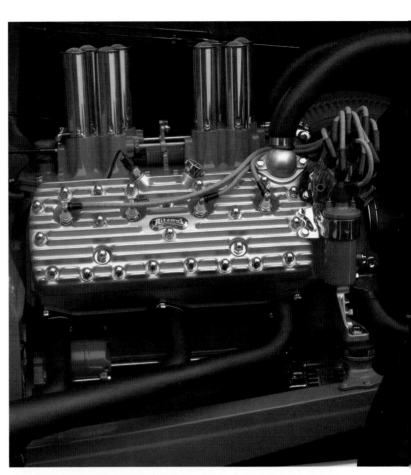

arry Lobeck, whose father was a serious hot rodder, grew up in rural Springfield, Ohio, with a passion for things mechanical. In 1983, he quit working as an assembler at International Harvester to open Lobeck's V-8 Shop, with his wife Ginny. He insists Springfield's lack of sports teams—and every other diversion save stock cars, short track racing, and sprint cars—strongly influenced the development of local hot rods. "We had our own little version of *American Graffiti* going on here," Lobeck told *Rodder's Journal* writer, Joe Kress, "and that's what we were all raised with."

For years, there's been a definite "Ohio Look," with Lobeck as the prime practitioner. His proven approach to coupes and roadsters began with eye-catching wheels and tires (always ETIII's or Americans, with fat Firestone dirt trackers on the back and skinny 135 or 145:15 Michelins in front), deep-dropped axles, reversed-eye springs, a well-defined rake, a serious chop, and nothing superfluous to a clean appearance. "Stance is key," Lobeck insists, along with close attention to fine detail. "My philosophy is that more is *not* better."

But things can change. The last three roadsters out of Lobeck's shop share their predecessors' elegant simplicity, but they're on skinnier tires—in one case, red-lines, with vintage-style instrument panels and old-style power plants. Lobeck clearly enjoys the synchronicity that develops between himself and his clientele. Take his distinctive '32 roadster with a Buick V-8 for Brad Arnold. "He came to me with just a Canadian Mercury Monarch hubcap and said, 'Let's build a car around this theme.' We talked about ideas, and I said, 'I'm thinkin' Buick nailhead.' He'd already started building one."

Unlike builders who remain focused on a narrow theme, Lobeck readily thinks out of the box. A stunning black Deuce cabriolet, done a few years ago, remains one of his favorite cars. "That car started the Dearborn Deuce business," he says with obvious pleasure. "I went up to visit those guys, and they were taking measurements from a life-size photograph." '32 cabriolets were rarely hot-rodded, but that didn't deter him. "That car showed people a cabriolet could be as neat a hot rod as a roadster. We canted the windshield posts back and cleaned it up, but we didn't have to do much to it to make it cool."

Although he loves doing Deuces, Lobeck can turn out a wide variety of car types. "I try to make the customer come to me. Once I know what he likes, I can do the right car for him." He has plenty of high-profile clients, including Keith Crain, George Poteet, and Sam Magarino, but "I try to treat everybody the same. George is one of the best," Lobeck adds. "He won't watch over you. He lets you cut your own throat.

"The great thing about George is that he instantly recognizes a good idea. I told him I always wanted to do a 'short-top' '40 convertible. He liked the idea and said if I did it, he'd buy it." Lobeck's phantom '40 creation uses an entire '40 DeLuxe front clip mated with a '40 coupe back end. The headlights and "wide five" wheels, reinterpreted in billet, are based on a '39 Ford. So is the single-seat interior. The windshield posts are laid back a scosch (it's neatly chopped) for a sleek silhouette. The dash is adapted from a '40, and there's no air, no heater, and no stereo. "This car just profiles so nice," Lobeck enthuses. "You could say it's the '40 that Ford should've built." You could add that it's something no one else has ever done as well.

One of Lobeck's star cars in the last few years was a radical '37 Ford cabriolet for Sam Magarino that resembles some of the classic pre-war custom German Fords created by coachbuilders like Spohn or Drauz. "Sam wanted a bigger car, and he wanted a custom. I showed him renderings of '40s-era Harry Westergard–style cars," Lobeck said, "but he didn't like that approach. Sam owns a dealership, so this car turned into a '90s custom, proving we don't do the same thing every time." With its artfully dipped beltline, recessed body reveal, exquisite aluminum side molding, ultra-low padded top, concept-car interior, full-length center console, and big-block motivation, Magarino's stunning '37 was a solid Ridler contender that became a reliable driver after its exhibition. "It drives like a Lexus," adds Lobeck.

Lobeck is currently working on a very clever '33 Ford cabriolet that's distinguished by an extended hood and a discretely narrowed '37 Ford truck grille. "I've always liked Jake's [Jim Jacobs'] yellow '34," Lobeck says, referring to the coupe that pioneered the use of this popular Ford commercial component. "But I thought the grille should be much thinner. We've extended the side reveal into the grille edge, for a cleaner beauty line that looks as though it came from the factory. We've laid the windshield posts back and fabricated a low top. This way, the car doesn't look so fat. And we've altered the frame to have the flavor of a '32 frame with that side reveal. Inside, it's plain and simple, with a center cluster adapted from a '50 Olds, twin glove boxes, hidden switches, and much more.

"This car got a little out of hand, dollar-wise. We put a lot of hours into getting the front splash pans right. But if you don't do it right," he asks, underscoring one of his prime tenets, "then why do it at all? I already had the car visualized, and I try to keep within budgets. But when you start getting into that handmade stuff, the hours increase and the price goes up."

Lobeck's shop created another memorable Ridler Award contender for Sam Magarino for the hotly contested 2007 Detroit Autorama. He brought a highly imaginative Thom Taylor design to life with a unique body that was crafted by Marcel Delay and Sons at Marcel's Custom Metal. If you try to picture a '40 Ford DeLuxe front clip on a '32 Ford roadster, with a DuVall-style windshield, on a completely custom tubular chassis, with hand-crafted and polished, fully independent suspension with adjustable coilovers, your mind probably hiccups. But as wild as it sounds, Barry and his team absolutely made it work.

This unique car exemplifies the Herculean conceptual and "dream car" executional efforts required of a Ridler contender these days. The fantastic gold '40 made the cut for the "Great 8," and it won a remarkable seven awards at Cobo Hall, but it was edged out by Ross and Beth Myers' sensational *First Love* '36 Ford coupe, created by Troy Trepanier at Rad Rods by Troy. "Sam said to me, 'Why didn't we win?' and I said, 'We were about $1.8 million short.' Even if a guy gave us a purse like Troy had, to build *this* car, I don't know how much better we could have done it.

"By the way," Lobeck adds proudly, "that '40 has been cleaning up on the show circuit. It was on the cover of *Street Rod Builder*. It won Darrell Starbird's show in Tulsa. And it's won 'Best Rod' practically everywhere it's been shown."

> ❝ *Stance is key, along with close attention to fine detail. My philosophy is that more is not better.* ❞

And it all started with a Thom Taylor rendering. "Thom Taylor and I both worked at International Harvester," Lobeck explains. "He worked in Fort Wayne. I met him at a rod run in Springfield. Pretty soon he was sending me pictures of stuff like the Vern Luce coupe. We became good friends, and we work very well together. I can tell Thom what I'm thinking, and the sketches will come back just right."

Lobeck doesn't see any lessening of demand for new cars, but he sees prices steadily escalating. "Used to be that nine out of ten cars were fiberglass; now it's the other way around. Brookville steel bodies aren't that much more expensive. Fiberglass bodies, like those Coast-to-Coast roadsters and similar cars, are OK for guys just starting out. But once you really get into this, you want steel. And you don't have to restore an old original car. That American Speed '34 roadster body is a helluva deal. Years ago, an entry-level car was twenty grand. Now it's tough to get something good for sixty. And if you get into something for the show circuit with a Marcel custom body, you're way into six figures."

Although his shop has been known for its older cars, Lobeck won't hesitate to do a newer model. "We did a '66 Corvette roadster," he says, "without hurting the body. It was very detailed, with the suspension done up right, and it's a very drivable car. And we did a '55 Chevy convertible, but we're so busy with hot rods, we haven't done as many of those.

"For me, the neat thing about doing all these cars is that I don't have to *own* them. And I like working with the same customers over and over again. I've got guys that come back two, three, even four times for new cars. I really like customers who'll just let us go. Some builders say 'Hit 'em hard, the first time.' Not me; I want to *keep* 'em coming back. *That's* how you build a business."

Speaking about other hot rod builders, Lobeck is quick to add, "We're all friends. And all these guys have their own special customers. Maybe a few of us are building a car for George Poteet. I had a guy come to me who was one of Ray Bartlett's [The Hot Rod Garage, Denton, Maryland] customers. So I called Ray to make sure if I did the work, there'd be no hard feelings. It was OK with him, so we did it.

"Once you get a good relationship with a customer, you can toss ideas back and forth. Some guys will say 'Lemme run this by you,' and they do, and you might tell 'em no, but if you've got the right guy, with the right momentum, the process continues. You've got to be true to a theme. You don't put billet mirrors on a traditional car. You do what you do well. And they respect you for it. That's why they came in the first place.

"After all these years, this is still enjoyable," he says. "We've got two locations; we build Just-A-Hobby chassis, and we have a big parts business, so it's a lot of work. I'm really no better than the guys we have working here. And we have a really good crew. My wife Ginny has a lot of input, too.

"Another thing," he is quick to add, "if a car can't be driven, we won't build it. You've got to be able to drive a car from one end of the country to the other. It's not all about trophies."

1937 FORD CONVERTIBLE CLUB COUPE
owned by Sam Magarino

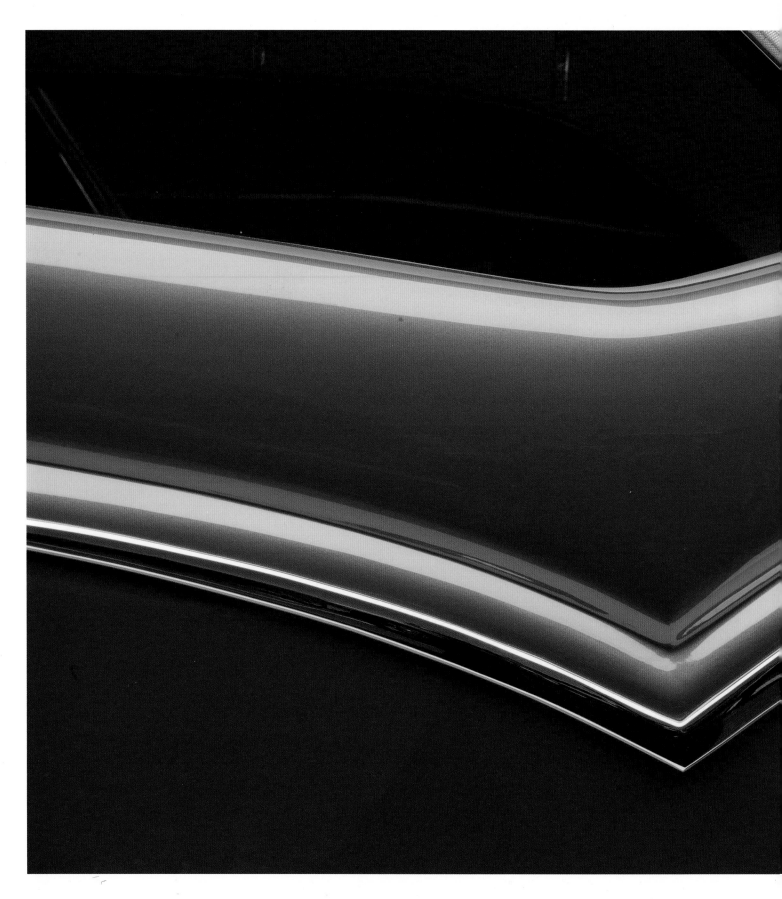

1932 FORD ROADSTER owned by Anthony Julian

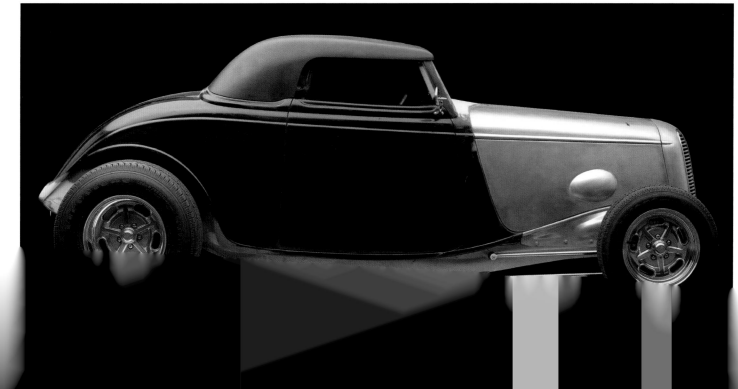

CHAPTER 9

RICK DORE
Art and Color Exemplified

Rick Dore is a fierce-looking guy with gunfighter eyes, sleeves of tattoos, and rock-solid credentials. His Glendale, Arizona, shop is as unpretentious as its output is unparalleled. Elected to four Custom Car Halls of Fame, he's won countless awards. Subtly elaborating on classic themes, Dore enhances them with his own distinctive melding of past and future elements.

"I worked out of my house for years and only opened my shop four years ago," he says, "although it's more like a studio than a shop. Before that, I was like a gypsy hustling between Phoenix and the Bay Area, working with talented guys like John Aiello and Bill Reasoner to build my cars."

Reflecting on his re-interpretation of the timeless Nick Matranga Mercury, he explains, "The '40 Merc is as good as it gets. I wanted to take this car a little further than Matranga did." With the hindsight of history, and inspired vision, Dore created a modern tribute. Taking things "a little further" is his mantra. He doesn't do clones, and he's not afraid to cut 'em up. Starting with an excellent donor prewar Mercury, Dore chopped the top four inches in front and six inches in back, then reshaped the entire roof line, creating a continuously rearward sweep. Elevating the windshield's height one inch, he trimmed the crown roof to eliminate the Matranga car's squinty, lowered-eyeshade appearance. The clean, subtly contemporary result respectfully paid homage to a long-lost car people revere, despite half a century.

Nobody in the custom car scene does this better.

To transform this pre-war beauty into a modern classic, the traditional twin spotlights were omitted. The chrome side-spear was re-sculpted and seductively shortened for a cleaner profile. The hand-formed taillights resemble art deco '40 Studebaker units, but they aren't actual Stude components. The coupe's elegant bumpers are devoid of any disruptions. Think illusion, impression, simplicity, dazzling finishes, and usually white interiors—but don't think pattern or sameness. He never does the same exact car twice.

Carrying the cool theme to the max, the front and rear fenders were molded; the running boards were trimmed and the skirts were flush-fitted, with discrete lower edge flares. The hood ornament, door, and decklid handles were shaved. The bodywork is all metal and flawless, as you'd expect. This car's gleaming, iridescent finish is unmistakably the art of Rick Dore; it's his signature. Translucent lime hues enhance every styling nuance. Inside, inviting front bucket and rear bench seats were trimmed in soft Italian white pearl leather, complimented by a console that was accented to match the exterior.

Dore's long skein of retro-inspired customs, like this stunning Mercury, represents an enduring design and styling statement; his cars' superb craftsmanship and his use of bright, very appealing shades are infinitely better-executed than the somber work done a half-century ago. "I used to do my cars in the Westergard style," he says, "and I've done some traditional '50s-style customs, but I'm not really into sleds any more. I'd prefer to take what Detroit gave us and enhance its existing lines. Both Cadillac roadsters I built resemble concept cars, or maybe they're long-lost show cars, just discovered, that Detroit designers put away in storage. They borrow from the best of the past. I still like 'em slammed on the ground, though."

Rick is perhaps best known for his custom car creations, but a few years ago, a dazzling, iridescent lime '34 Ford roadster with molded and skirted '36 Ford rear fenders, the hit of the SEMA show, proved that he knows his way around early hot rods. "When that car was featured on the cover of *Street Rodder*, it opened up people's minds," says Dore. "Nobody expected it."

Show car publicist Michael Dobrin says, "Rick Dore has a restless and inventive spirit. He reaches out and goes where nobody has ever gone before."

We'd add that when Rick works on an existing theme, like the '60s-style Model T roadster he did with his daughter, Suzanne, he finds a way to do it differently. At the same time, his show-stopping work makes you wonder why no one thought of that particular approach before. At the 2007 SEMA show, Dore rolled in a '36 Ford roadster commissioned by Houston car collector John O'Quinn. '36 Fords and Duesenbergs don't usually appear in the same sentence, but Dore found a way to meld the pair, beginning with an elegant Harry Westergard–inspired (but totally different than anything on a Westergard car) vertical grille, distinctive side trim, candy paint you could reach deeply into, and a gentle rearward slope that said "taildragger," without its dragging its tail.

One of the things Rick Dore does best is to reach into the past, find a classic everyone knows, then take a fresh car and integrate those old themes, with many subtle updates. The result is at once familiar, and nothing ever seen before. On a recent shop visit, Rick had two partially completed projects that underscored this practice. One was a nasty-looking '37 Ford coupe that he's been building for Metallica guitarist James Hetfield. Chopped and severely lowered, with a reshaped hood and skirted rear fenders, this "mean streets" bad boy evokes memories of speeding cars and teenaged outlaws popularized in 1950s B-movies. Last year, he completed a stunning custom Buick Riviera for Hetfield. "James definitely knows what he wants, and I give him a little guidance when he needs it."

For O'Quinn, Dore has taken a pristine '61 Lincoln, slammed it to within an inch of the deck, transformed it into a convertible, chopped the windshield, and reshaped only that original trim he felt was absolutely necessary to improve the car's execution. "I showed a rendering to O'Quinn that Jimmy Smith did. He took one look and said, 'We've got to do this car.' He likes my style; there's a mutual trust factor, and I appreciate having him for a client. I've done cars for John that went from my shop right to his museum. Very few people have seen them."

A proud co-founder of the famed "Beatniks" car club, Dore appreciates his club's special camaraderie. "Everybody has a sharper edge," he says. "Whether the members are from the U.S., Japan, or Australia, these aren't guys in flamed sneakers. They're very talented. And yeah, many of us have tattoos. We only meet a few times a year, in El Paso, or at the San Francisco Rod & Custom Show. It's not open to everybody—just 40 or so guys."

Many builders covet the America's Most Beautiful Roadster (AMBR) and Ridler awards, but not Rick Dore. "The Ridler, in particular, has gotten way out of hand," he says. "Sure the winners are beautiful—they're rolling art—but they're multi-million-dollar cars. There's no basis in reality anymore. I've won everything else, some of them a few times. It's somebody else's turn now—maybe it's whoever buys one of my cars. Not being a body man, I'm in a unique position. Luckily, I've gotten to work with some great guys who let me tell them how I want it done, and they go along with me."

Dore's imaginative use of color is unique and unmistakable. "I like soft pastels, pearls, and candies," he says. "Again, I'm fortunate that some of the best painters in the business, like Art Himsl, let me fool around in their shops. So I'll come up with a shade, something I'll mix myself, and they'll figure out how to make 100 times as much. My inspiration comes from everywhere. I was in a little flea market south of Rome a few years ago, and a guy from Africa was selling stones. I looked at one of them, and there was the green shade for that '34. To me, color is 99 percent. It has to draw you to the car. *Then* you look at the details."

95

1950 HUDSON HARDTOP COUPE
owned by Don and Flo Macofski

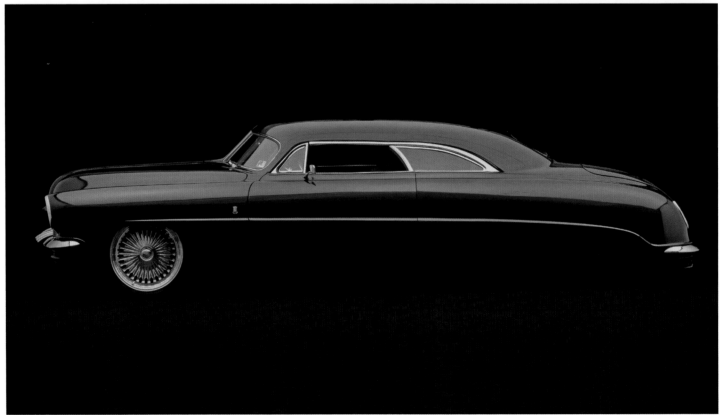

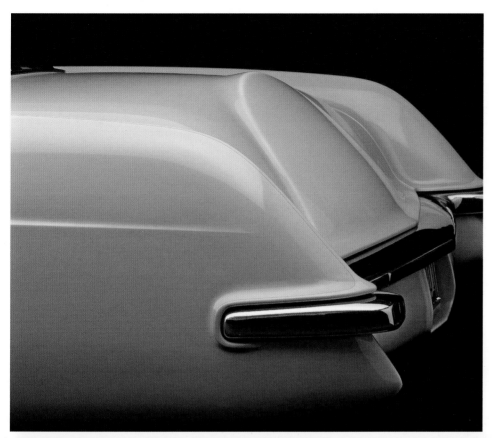

1937 FORD FIVE-WINDOW COUPE owned by James Hetfield

1951 MERCURY HARDTOP COUPE

owned by Rick Dore

CHAPTER 10

DAVE CROUSE
"Bringing Them Back Alive"

Dave Crouse's shop, Custom Auto, is about 45 minutes from Denver, but when you see the cars being worked on there, you'd think you were in Southern California in the 1950s. Dave's dad owned Harmony Speedway in Harmony, New Jersey, across the river from the Andretti stronghold of Nazareth, Pennsylvania, and as a kid he absolutely loved cars. "There were many racetracks close by, like Flemington, New Jersey, and Middletown, New York's Orange County Speedway. I was always tagging along."

Raised on a farm and mechanically adept, Dave started his first hot rod, a Model T, when he was 13. "I worked with an older man who taught me all about being a purist," he recalls. "We restored a 1917 Model T together, and when it was finished, we *drove* it to Hershey." Later, Crouse worked on classics and sports cars at Stone Barn Auto Restoration in Vienna, New Jersey, but his heart was always in hot rods. In the late '80s, he moved to Colorado. "There were still lots of old cars out here," he recalls, "and I had the right contacts to find them."

"But I wanted to get my own shop," he says, "so I did whatever it took to get started—machine work, working on other kinds of cars, etc." He developed a good reputation, bought his present location in 1995, and received a big break with the restoration of the long-lost, ex–Joe Nitti *Deep Purple* '32 roadster. "David Zivot snookered me into the Nitti car," he says, not unkindly. "I was determined to get into that kind of historic hot rod." Custom Auto's meticulous and accurate restoration of this seminal roadster won the coveted Bruce Meyer Preservation Award at the 2000 Grand National Roadster Show. With the resulting acclaim, Dave and his crew were on their way.

Crouse's friend and collector Roger Morrison likes to collect old hot rods with interesting histories, underwrite their restoration, then reunite the cars with their former owners. The effect on these old hot rodders, who are surprised someone even *remembers* their efforts after fifty years, is extraordinary. That's what happened with the ex–Bud Neumeister Model A, a *Hot Rod* magazine cover car back in 1954.

After Dave and his Custom Auto crew completely restored the A/V-8, Roger arranged an historic meeting between Bud Neumeister and former NHRA President and ex–*Hot Rod* magazine editor Wally Parks at the 2004 Grand National Roadster Show. The two last corresponded fifty years ago, when the story of Bud's home garage build-up appeared in *Hot Rod* over two issues. They'd never actually met. When the elderly duo shook hands and embraced, they were both elated and teary. So was everyone present.

Roger Morrison saw the ex–Berardini Brothers drag-race championship-winning "404" roadster for the first time at the Grand National Roadster Show in 2004, and he made owner Rudy Perez an offer he couldn't refuse. It was soon on its way to Crouse's shop in Loveland, Colorado, for a frame-off restoration. Crouse received a street roadster that didn't resemble the old 404 at all, but he didn't have to work in a vacuum. Morrison videotaped Pat Berardini and collected many period photos to learn construction details of the now much-altered roadster.

Studying old pictures and talking to Pat Berardini, Crouse and his shop slowly brought the 404 back to life. "This car had a continuous in-use history for more than half a century," says Crouse. "But there were many missing parts. Mike Spacek and Jim Stroupe helped us find things that almost don't exist. Roger has a tremendous commitment to professional work. Restoring his cars, honoring these hot rod heroes, is a real pleasure."

"Roger insisted we repair and use as much of the original frame as we could," Crouse continues, "even though we both knew it would be more time-consuming and expensive to unbox a chassis that had seen considerable changes over the years. We replaced the front frame horns, and most of the rear sections behind the cross-member. I tried to talk Roger out of that at first, but he insisted. He wanted a 'no-excuses' car.

"It was a very challenging restoration. We got a replacement flathead block, bored it 1/8th over, and installed a new SCAT four-inch crank and 8CM rods. We didn't jack up the compression too much. I have a trick for those four carburetors, so they all open and close simultaneously, they'll idle, and they'll pull smoothly. It runs so great it really baffles people. Flatheads are my specialty," he says modestly.

Ed Iskenderian personally pulled his last 404 camshaft and lifters off the shelf to ensure the born-again flathead would have that legendary cam with its characteristically rough idle and sharp throttle response. Says Crouse, "This car had to have a 404 cam. They're not easy to find, but we'd never have done it any other way."

"But you need a committed client," he says, "and Roger's a joy to work for. It's a fantasy come true to be able to do cars like this and show our talent." Adds Morrison, "At Dave's shop, everybody, even the younger guys, has an appreciation for history. They're passing it on to the next generation."

Custom Auto's restoration of the Pate Brothers *Bell 303* competition roadster was featured in *Hot Rod* magazine. Dave says the 303 was "basically complete," but it was in "terrible condition."

"One of the great things about a client like Roger," Crouse says, "is his appreciation for history. On the ex–Bell 303, he encouraged us to use as much of the original body and frame as we could to ensure authenticity." During restoration, the brothers supplied photographs, old films of the car competing, and advice for Crouse and his crew.

After a lengthy rebuild, Crouse was filmed testing the 303 on its maiden voyage, the first time since

1954 that the car was underway under its own power. The Isky 404-cammed flathead crackled with power, and one could only imagine what it must have been like, blasting off the line at Santa Ana or Bakersfield. Crouse located an original set of Bruce slicks, with a shipping tag still extant that read "Waltner Electric, Moundridge, KS." Ordered half a century ago, stored away, and never used, they were just waiting for this project. Crouse is a pro at finding that stuff.

Custom Auto is currently restoring the ex–Chet Herbert *Beast IV* streamliner for David Duthu. "I love to do the research on these cars," Crouse says. "If I didn't have to make a living, that's *all* I'd do. We call it 'automotive archaeology.'" Dave learned his research skills from his friend, the late Bruce Craig of Phillipsburg, New Jersey, a racecar aficionado whose persistent search for historic accuracy inspired Crouse to urge another client, Steve Memishian, to establish the American Hot Rod Foundation.

> ❝ *First, you've got to choose the most important time period, the one that's just right for that car, and then restore it to match.* ❞

"The only way you should start with cars like the Herbert streamliner is with research," says Crouse. "First, you've got to choose the most important time period, the one that's just right for *that* car, and then restore it to match. You have to decide how much of the car is worth saving and how much of it needs new parts. You also have to look at how the restored car will be used. With the Bell 303 roadster, we installed a couple of period-correct vintage water tanks so Roger could drive the car for the race car test at the AACA National Meet in Hershey. With the Chet Herbert car, it'll have to be high enough to go over the ramp at Pebble Beach."

At any time, there could be a dozen cars under restoration at Custom Auto. "It's a juggling act," says Crouse. We do a round robin, waiting for parts, waiting while we research a car's history, waiting for machine work . . . fortunately, I have a fabulous crew. It's hard to find a group of guys like this who share your philosophy, but I've got 'em. We all enjoy what we're doing. When we went to Pebble Beach with the Berardini roadster (it won the Dean Batchelor Award in 2007 for the most significant restored hot rod), I wanted all my guys to be there, to experience the world's best car show and to appreciate all its aspects."

As Custom Auto's reputation for doing historic cars has grown, they've received rare commissions.

"Gary Cerveny brought us the ex–Norman Timbs, rear-engine, Buick-powered custom," Crouse says. "We've got a lot of period photos to help us do it right, including ones of the wooden body buck. I knew about this car when it was up in the high desert; then it disappeared, then went to the Petersen Museum. Gary bought it, did the research, realized he was in over his head, and brought it to us. So I got it to do anyway."

The shop is restoring the ex–Larry Shinoda *Chopsticks Special* Deuce three-window for Ross Myers. "That was another decision," says Crouse, "because that car had two great early histories and an even longer life when it was campaigned by Don Montgomery. We're going to take it back to the Shinoda period; Ross admires Larry and his design of the Corvette Sting Ray, but when it's finished, we'll do a clone of the Montgomery coupe for Ross."

"I'm still looking for some of the great cars, and I know where some of the missing ones are," he says cryptically, naming just enough lost metal to pique my curiosity. "They just can't be bought yet for various reasons. Meanwhile, although it's in rough shape, we're researching a '51 Chevy custom we've got, and we're doing a Matranga Mercury re-creation for David Zivot."

Is there a secret to Custom Auto's success? "Having good people around you is key," says Crouse. "I don't do this by myself. Great clients are essential; so's the media. There's a kinship of people who are interested in these historic cars. I tell my guys they may not get rich, but we're living in a great place, bringing great cars back to life. My crew calls me 'the old man,'" he says with a chuckle, "and they ask when I'm going to retire. I tell 'em I retired when I started this business."

1932 FORD ROADSTER owned by Jorge Zaragoza

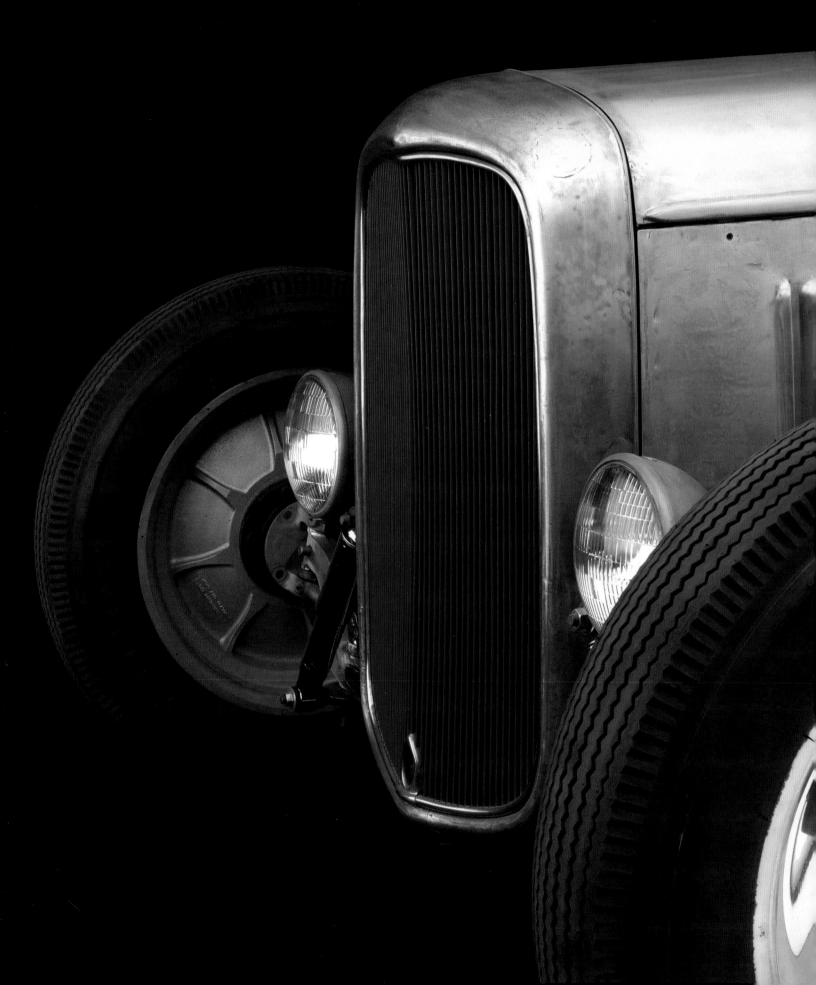

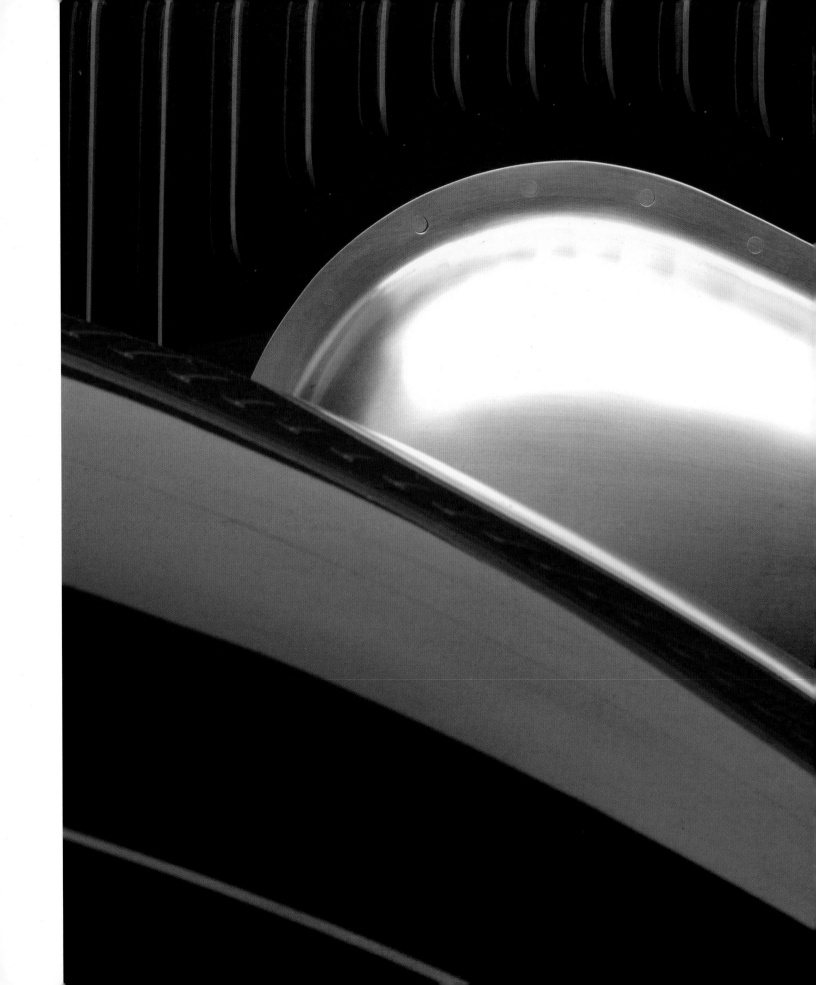

1929 FORD MODEL A ROADSTER, EX–BUD NEUMEISTER

owned by Roger Morrison

1932 FORD ROADSTER owned by Dave Crouse

1927 FORD *BELL 303 CRANKSHAFT SPECIAL*

owned by Roger Morrison

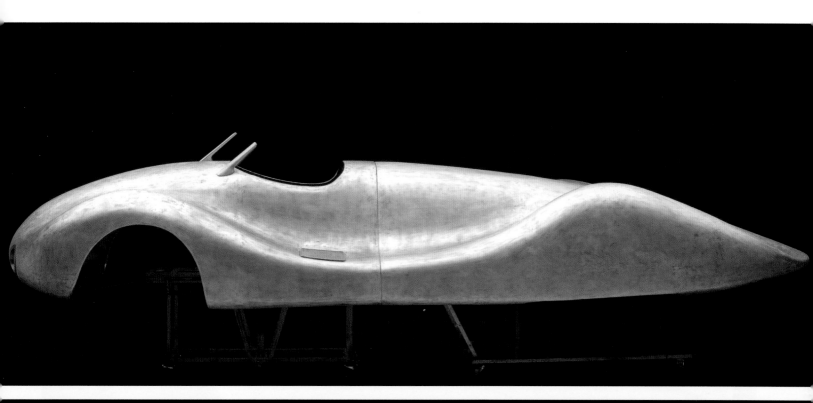

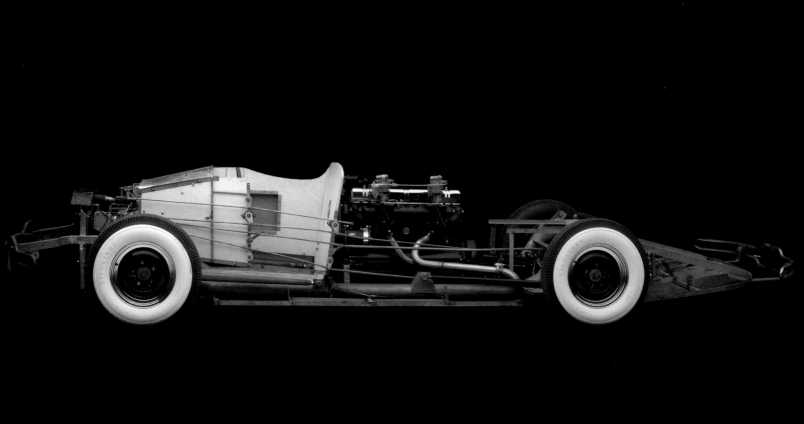

1948 CUSTOM, EX–NORMAN TIMBS owned by Gary Cerveny

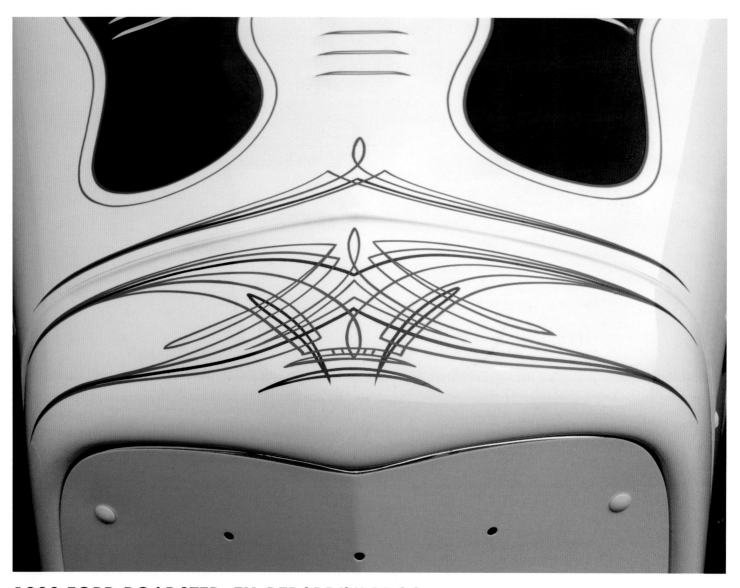

1932 FORD ROADSTER, EX–BERARDINI BROS. owned by Roger Morrison

"I guess if you stay with something long enough, it'll come back around again," builder Donn Lowe observes. A dyed-in-the-wool advocate of mid-century custom and hot rod aesthetics and of old-world craftsmanship, he's a preservationist. A self-described "ultra-traditionalist," it's tempting to write him off as being trapped in the '50s.

But to do so would miss his point. As a builder, Lowe's brand of preservation isn't simply the regurgitation of old and trusted themes. Instead, it's a pragmatic philosophy based on his desire to keep traditional aesthetics and philosophies from stagnating. Lowe looks carefully in his rearview mirror, even as he drives resolutely into the future. Operating out of Lowe Kustoms, his professional-grade home shop in Oregon City, Oregon, Lowe and his two-man crew put a spin on the traditional rod and custom aesthetic with each car they build.

For example, a few years back, while working from Harry Bentley Bradley designs, they crafted a stunning '40 Mercury convertible for John Babcock that embraces traditional and contemporary elements while evading classification as either one. Rather than take our word that Lowe's efforts don't suffer the "neither fish-nor-fowl" syndrome endemic among most cars that try to bridge that gap, know that this car won the 2005 Barris Custom d'Elegance award, one of the most esteemed honors in the custom-car world.

"You could call it a modern tribute to the Jimmy Summers Mercury (memorialized in Dan Post's *Blue Book of Custom Restyling*)," Lowe said, "but it's different in every way. I loved the old Summers car, and I wanted to do something like it. Harry Bradley worked on this design from the beginning. He said, and I agree, there's 'no sense in re-popping what has already been done.'"

"Harry had sent me pictures of Jimmy's Mercury with little notes on details. In the 1940s, that car was incredible, but by the 1990s, it was dated. The new car has a certain sweep to it, and that was all Harry's doing. Really the whole look is Harry's."

When you see the new Mercury, you can't help but be impressed by its long, tapering hood line. "The firewall is still in the stock location," Lowe explains. But to execute Bradley's concept, Lowe thinned out the vertical section between the hood cut line and the cowl, from side to side. The cowl vent was removed, and the windshield posts were chopped three inches, moved three inches rearward, and angled inward 15 degrees. The center post and the side windows were then cut to match, and the upper windshield frame was sectioned, about half its width for a thinner appearance. The cowl itself was stretched three inches to the rear, lengthening the hood. While the hood was reworked with metal taken from the original, it, too, was largely handmade.

The passenger "cell" was moved three inches rearward, along with the "B" pillars. A new floor and subrails are all handmade as well. The tops of the doors were modified to curve upward toward the windshield, and the rear door corners have been rounded. A removable "Carson style" top was completely formed in foam at first, in order to determine the final shape. Next, a plaster mold was made and laid up in fiberglass over a tubular steel framework. The resulting top shape is exquisite. It's a critical detail that's too often fluffed.

This car's front fenders are three inches longer as well, and beautifully rolled and molded into the quarter panel. The wheel wells have been moved up three inches, and the wheel openings are an inch and a half higher, radiused to match the tops of the wheels. A discrete set of low fadeaways tapers back from the front to the rear fenders. The bottoms of the doors had to be shortened about an inch so they would open above the fadeaway line and not cut intrusively into it. Handmade rocker panels completed this arduous task. There's not much on this car that hasn't benefited from Harry Bradley's keen eye, some input from Dave Crook, and most importantly, the profound metalworking skills of Lowe.

It sounds simple, but the entire supporting structure underneath the doors had to be completely redesigned and fabricated to accommodate the many changes. Although it looks as though it's even lower than the Summers car because its ground clearance is less, the Babcock Mercury's body was "only" channeled an inch and a half. The result, more attractive and better balanced than the old car's, is reminiscent of proportions beloved by classic French carrossiers (coachbuilders) like Figoni and Falaschi, on Delages and Delahayes.

Unlike Summers' car, where the side trim was completely removed, this new edition has a unique, custom-designed accent that runs neatly along the body reveal. It was hand-formed in brass, then plated. The elegant side trim tapers from a thin line along the hood to a wider feature line, really a discrete slash across the door. The resulting slightly dipped effect lends a distinct sense of movement, even when the car is sitting still.

The hood had to be cut and pancaked to fit, and it's flared ever so slightly where it surrounds the grille. On the Summers car, the hood was flattened and the fenders were raised, leaving the front fenders more prominent than they needed to be to achieve the desired result. Lowe approached the challenge of lowering this car differently, using contemporary modifications like Heidt's Airide tubular independent front suspension and an adjustable airbag system so the car can be raised and lowered.

"I might be an ultra-traditionalist, but I try to push the envelope," Lowe explains. "I love to do traditional cars with features that *could've* been done back then but never were." For example, when he built what's now Buddy Pepp's *Washington Blue Deuce* roadster, he changed its dash. But instead of going for the usual art deco '40 Ford panel, he skillfully fitted one from a '51

Chevrolet passenger car. "You never would've seen that done in the '50s," he admits, "but you look at it and you go, 'Whoa, why didn't *that* come on?'"

Imbued with 1950s sensibilities ("I had this childhood that was straight out of *Leave it to Beaver*," he recalls) and formally trained in auto body repair as part of an official apprenticeship program ("You could call it learning the classical way," he said. "I was taught how to straighten metal and work with lead."), Lowe brought a unique set of skills to the collision-repair business that springboarded his career. Though his particular high level of craftsmanship put Lowe ahead of his peers, one could make the case that it impaired his value in the evolving collision-repair industry.

"By the early eighties, for example, I could see the handwriting on the wall as far as the collision business was concerned," Lowe recalls. "It went from straightening and getting a lot of labor time to just parts replacement." Rather than conceding defeat, though, he returned to his roots. "I told my wife, 'I want to open a custom shop,'" he muses, chuckling. "Of course, that was in '82, and when I look back on it, it was *really* stupid."

But, thank goodness, hindsight follows experience. Since striking out on his own some 26 years ago, Lowe's merged his interests and skills, tempering them with a dose of historical perspective. And by many accounts, it's worked. "I've been very lucky to hook up with several guys as clients who allow me to build some neat cars," he acknowledges.

> ❝ *I might be an*
> *ultra-traditionalist,*
> *but I try to push*
> *the envelope.* ❞

"Like right now we're doing a '40 coupe for Doug Beattie that's along the lines of [John Babcock's] '40 Mercury as far as the amount of work that'll go into it," he says. Drawing from his historical interests, "It's pre-war European design; we moved the passenger cell to the rear, thereby lengthening the nose. It looks like it could've been a prototype for a really zootie Lincoln," Lowe enthuses.

"Doug and I just happen to be exactly in the same groove. It's almost like we speak to each other through telepathy; we just *know* what each other likes." For example, "I'd come up with ideas and he'd say, 'Oh, that's *exactly* what I was thinking.' The windshield on this '40 is extremely raked; the car's sectioned and channeled. Even though it retains the same wheelbase and it's close to the same overall length, it looks about twice as long as a typical '40 Ford."

He's quick to point out that a builder, no matter how talented, is merely a figure in an equation. "To

build a car like this, of course, takes a lot more time and money. There are many different ways to get a car to look the way you want it to look. You can wire weld and use Bondo for about a third of the time, but we simply don't do that. We try to be a cut above. Everything we do here is metal-shaped. It's leaded. We do it that way because it's forever, and the price reflects that level of work. So what you've done by maintaining a standard like that is eliminate eight out of ten guys (as clients) right off the bat. They can't afford it.

"What I'm looking for in a customer is the one guy who knows the difference, appreciates that effort, and wants that [kind of car] for his collection. I learned that from Mike McKenett (of Restorations and Reproductions, with whom Lowe worked between 1988 and '92). He's an engineer, which also helps out a lot. Mike is a guy whose workmanship I really admire. I've learned a lot from him. Because of that experience, we simply try to build a *really* superb car."

Despite being a proponent of exotic and highly finished cars, Lowe is quick to recognize his own roots. Drawing from what some may consider an unlikely inspiration, "I think the so-called rat-rod thing—I wish there was a better name for it—that whole low-dollar, foot-wetting thing, is terrific. What an absolutely *great* way for young guys to get into this stuff. If you look at a lot of bare-metal cars, and the chassis they're building, these cars are *cool*. These kids have started this whole new look by taking a pickup cab and slamming it over a chassis and throwing a tank on the back. It's this generation's answer to what this stuff should be. They've got the look *down*."

It's when Lowe talks about the future of the hobby that he really starts showing the progressive side of his philosophy. "Hot rodding has always been leading the pack, or at least following closely behind. I'm a realist; I understand that the days [of the gasoline engine] are numbered, but it doesn't mean there won't be any more '32 roadsters. As soon as the technology has been developed and is available, there'll be some enterprising hot rodder who will put that platform under an old car."

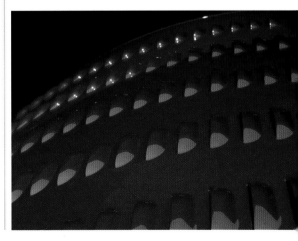

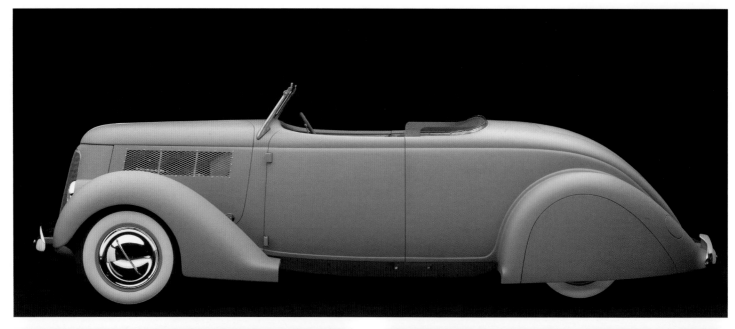

1936 FORD ROADSTER owned by Creighton Helms

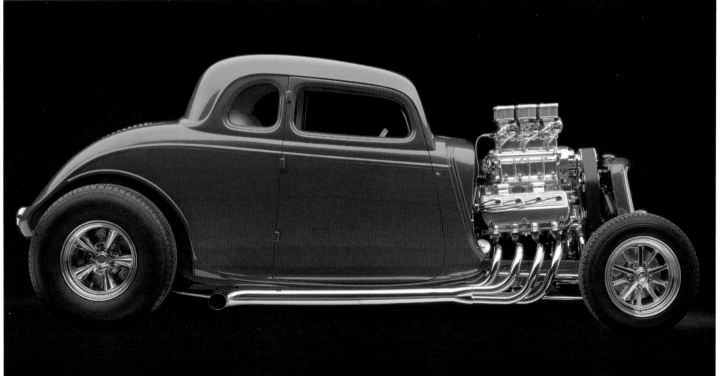

1934 FORD FIVE-WINDOW COUPE *BLUTO* owned by Doug Beattie

1951 CHEVROLET BEL AIR HARDTOP owned by Rory Craner

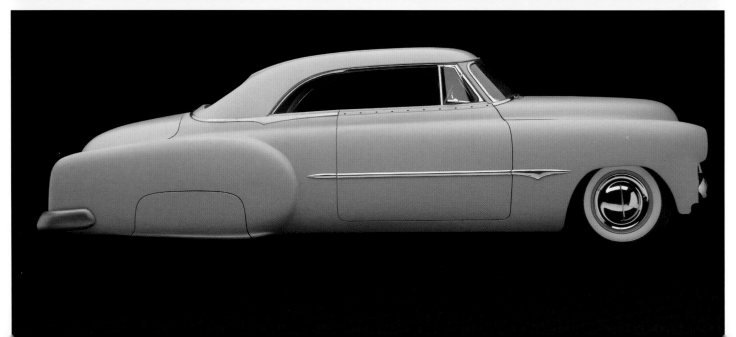

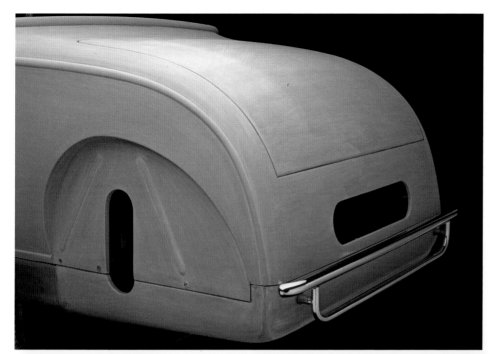

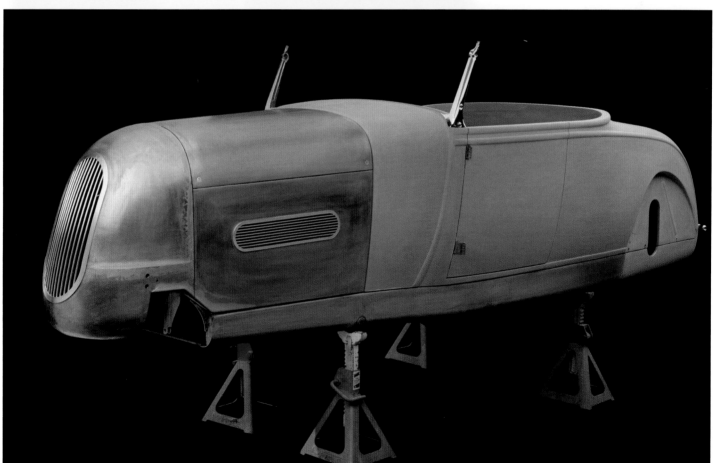

CHAPTER 12

STEVE FRISBIE
Transcendental Mechanization

The custom car and hot rod world generate many wonderful paradoxes, many old designs set lasting precedents, and even ordinary elements can become exceptional. If there's a consistent theme, it's that objects catalyzed by the genre often emerge as the very opposite of what they originally represented.

At the forefront of that movement, you'll find Steve's Auto Restorations (SAR), a 14,000-square-foot shop in Portland, Oregon. Owner Steve Frisbie is one of those intriguing paradoxes. As indicated by his shop's name, he's a restorer first and foremost, but he's proven repeatedly that he's not afraid of taking a torch to a coach-built car. Although Frisbie's an ardent art deco buff, SAR has received much of its acclaim after several projects that helped establish the extreme-restyling trend that defines the new millennium's ultra-progressive look. That's what makes Frisbie a compelling influence: you never know what he'll do next.

To underscore the point, two of his cars immediately come to mind—Marshall Chesrow's and Dave Hall's radically customized Chevrolet Nomads. While Chesrow's *RealMad* started as a '56 model, after Chip Foose's design work and SAR's superb craftsmanship, its current lithe profile looks as if it were extruded that way. Not surprisingly, its sleek orange-and-black body retains a scant ten square feet of its original shape. Bear in mind that this car was done in an era when a chopped top on a model like this was considered a major undertaking.

Thanks to its restrained sophisticated lines, and Chris Ito's design talents, Hall's *NewMad* looks as if it could have emerged from a GM design studio. Remember, this was a car built in an era when today's big-name designers were little more than hot rod shop employees. This car is a unique expression, all the way to its hand-formed trim and bumpers—a shop specialty Frisbie proudly emphasizes. In many ways, the *NewMad* has come to represent his shop.

Both customs are the tip of the proverbial iceberg. In their wake are, among others, a dechromed, lowered, and simplified '64 Pontiac GTO imbued with street rod sensibilities; a coach-built '37 Ford so perfect in conception that it could make the European craftsmen at Karl Deutsch Karrosserie, who originally bodied it, bow with humility; and a stunning '57 Ford pickup, with a supercharged Cobra V-8 that won the 2006 Goodguys Truck of the Year award (and looks like the truck that FoMoCo *should've* built rather than the semi-predictable passenger-car-based production model that Ford introduced more than half a century ago).

So how does he do it?

Aside from a keen aesthetic and a dedicated staff, "I've got that organizational assembly-line mentality," Frisbie reflects. "It might go all the way back to my days at Boeing, where there's so much organization, and you see airplane parts move from the drawing board to the milling machine, on down the line to plating and paint." Frisbie still thinks in production and close inspection terms; thankfully, it's no longer mass production.

Though his own nearly vertically integrated production model creates a fertile bed for exotic projects like the Nomads to take seed, Frisbie's rationale for his success is a little more humble. "We see a lot of the mid-stream changes," he observes. "When a car gets shopped around, every time it goes to a new shop, that guy says, 'this is wrong and that's wrong and I'm going to have to redo this and fix that.' Well *that's* expensive.

"Now if you can do it all under one roof and the guy twenty feet away from you will be getting that fender when you're done with it, you have this interactive communication. These things can turn into thousands of hours, so even if you can save ten percent of redo, it's cost-effective in the long run. Of course, how do you say a million-dollar car is cost effective?" he asks, with a bit of ironic humor.

But as paradoxical as the notion of a cost-effective exotic car sounds, Frisbie maintains that the two ideas needn't necessarily contradict each other. For example, to prevent customers from squandering their money at every whim, "We try to do sketches and renderings. That practice will usually stop a 'bad' idea before much effort and money are expended."

Frisbie would rather see a client's funds used to extend the creative envelope. "We try to push people to the extent of their *imaginations*. If their wallet can handle it, we'll go there. If they can't, we'll go backwards on the design and radical theme. We listen an awful lot to what the client wants, then try to coach them along the way. Somehow you've got to understand that the philosophy [of watching cost] really *is* there."

There's a secondary reason for pre-planning and design, Frisbie admits, if not a little bit sheepishly. "I guess that I have a little more than just an interest in the art deco flavor in some of these cars. Even though I've got a shop manager and designer here full staff, I'm always trying to interject some deco [elements] into things. Sometimes they'll pull me back and say 'That's not for *this* client,' which sometimes it isn't," he says, chuckling. "I know it comes from my restoration days when I was doing [Mercedes-Benz] 540Ks, and Packards, and Cords, and Delahayes, and Daimlers, and early '30s Cadillacs and that kind of stuff."

While the shop has revisited its restoration roots recently, the work is not always to stock specifications. For example, they tended to body and paint chores as part of a restoration for former racer, Tom Gloy, of the ex–Ralph Jilek, chopped and channeled '40 Ford convertible. That car was a Pebble Beach–quality restoration (it took second place in the Early Custom Car Class in 2005), but rather than do the work to resemble an original Ford, it was finished to the era-correct, high standard that legendary builders Neil Emory and Clayton Jensen established more than half a century ago at their Valley Custom Shop in Burbank, California.

> 66 *We listen an awful lot to what the client wants, then try to coach them along the way. Somehow you've got to understand that the philosophy [of watching cost] really is there.* 99

Frisbie recently acquired, and is restoring, another seminal Valley Custom car: Ron Dunn's sectioned '50 Ford coupe. Likely the Burbank duo's most famous effort (certainly a personal favorite), Frisbie is adamant that this car is going back together exactly the way Neil and Clay intended it to look when it was completed in 1953.

Though we've highlighted many of Frisbie's intriguing paradoxes, his production model and custom-car mindset mesh perfectly in one area. In the late '90s, he created Real Steel with the intention of reproducing Ford bodies in steel. Starting by assembling Deuce bodies from Brookville roadster panels, Real Steel eventually tooled up to make a very correct '33–'34 roadster body of its own, as well as a unique '33–'34 roadster pickup design that Frisbie created. Both are assembled on precision fixtures, using modern welding techniques. They are arguably better built than anything that emerged from Ford's Rouge plant back in the day.

Galvanized by the success of the Model 40 roadster bodies and by Brookville's success with its own steel coupe body, Frisbie recently indulged in a fantasy of his own: reproducing Ford's three-window '33–'34 coupe. As we went to press, the coupe tooling—based on scans pulled from an unmolested example—has been finalized, and production is near. These bodies will be solid, 19-gauge steel, stamped by EMI in Detroit, and they will be meticulously assembled at SAR using modern welding techniques. "It's definitely going forward," Frisbie says with the enthusiasm of an expectant father. "We're going to have our first body ready for the 2008 Nats (the NSRA Street Rod Nationals in Louisville, Kentucky).

"We've got a couple of interesting marketing plans with that coupe," he reveals. Among them is a promotional "really big idea." He plans to build a one-off reproduction of Pete Chapouris' hammered '34 3W that's known as *The California Kid*, made famous in a made-for-TV movie starring Martin Sheen. He says, "Jerry Slover [steward of the namesake and present owner of Pete & Jake's Hot Rod Parts] has offered to let us have *The Kid* here in the shop so we can do a side-by-side clone."

Bridging old and new, Steve's Auto Restorations is also marketing all-steel '55 and '57 Chevy convertible bodies. Builders can mount one of these exact reproductions on a stock chassis, or SAR will provide a complete Art Morrison chassis. Many years ago, when Dee Wescott began the construction of fiberglass bodies, hot rodders embraced the change, and the sport expanded to be more accessible for a legion of hobbyists who either couldn't afford original steel cars, or, *if* they managed to locate an example, they didn't have the skills or couldn't afford the metal work it took to massage decades-old metal into something presentable. But there was always that oft-unspoken stigma about "glass" bodies, no matter how well they were made and reinforced. Seventy-five years later, you can buy a brand new, bare metal '32, '33, or '34 Ford roadster or coupe body that's better than original, and it's probably cheaper than you could buy a real one and restore it. Is this a great country or what?

Like most paradoxes, Frisbie evades classification. Is he a restorer or a customizer? A specialist or a manufacturer? A traditionalist or a modern technophile? A preservationist or a forward-thinker? Does he create tomorrow's idols, or is he simply an iconoclast?

The answer, I'm sure he'd tell you, is somewhere between all of them, and none of the above. I certainly wouldn't expect any less.

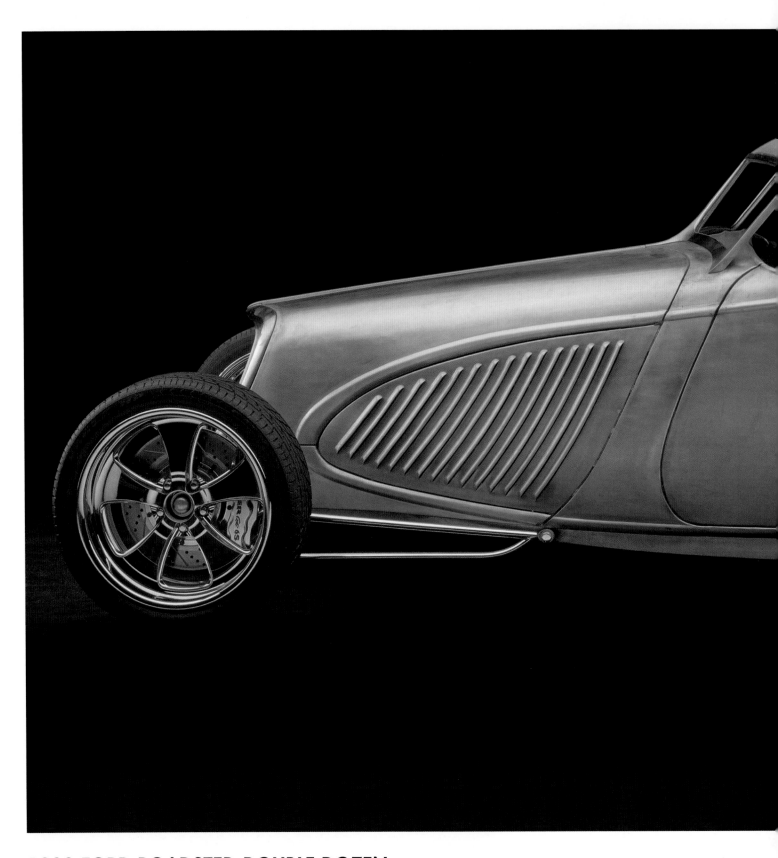

1933 FORD ROADSTER *DOUBLE DOZEN* owned by Steve Frisbie

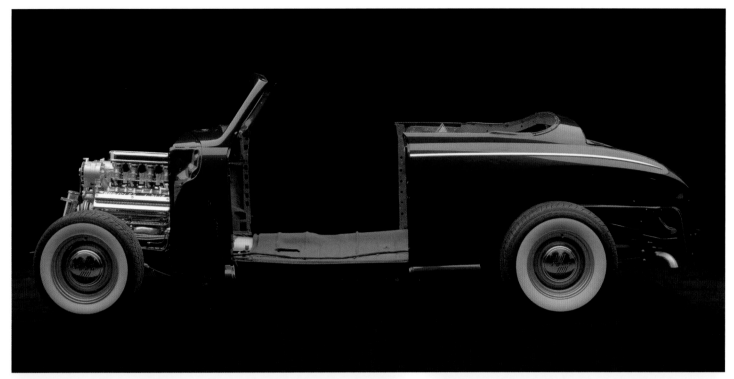

1946 FORD CONVERTIBLE owned by Dave Hall

1932 FORD ROADSTER owned by Bill Bauce

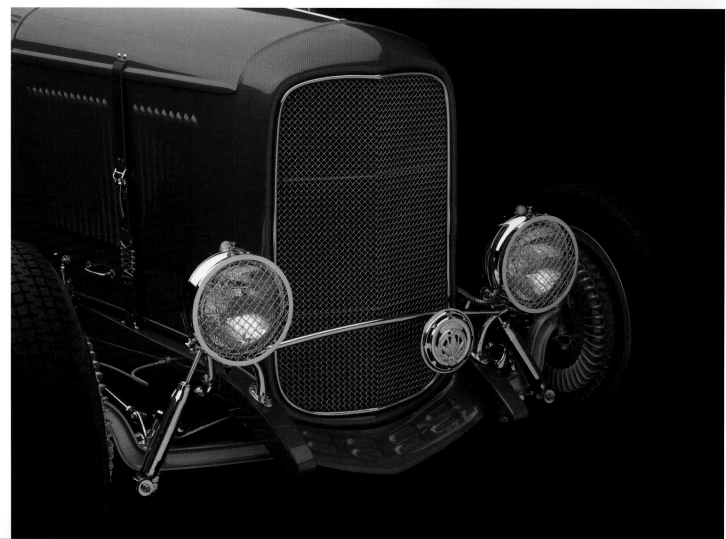

1933 DODGE PICKUP TRUCK owned by "Anonymous"

CHAPTER 13

DON OROSCO
The Relentless
Pursuit of Perfection

Don Orosco's well-equipped shop, near Laguna Seca Raceway in Monterey, California, is known for extraordinary restorations. But Orosco, a shopping center builder and developer (DBO Developments, Inc.), doesn't restore cars for others. His ever-growing personal collection provides plenty of work for his skilled craftsmen.

Competing at the Pebble Beach Concours d'Elegance on four occasions, Orosco and his talented team of Olle Ericksson, Brad Hand, and Jesse Cruz took third place in the inaugural Historic Hot Rod Class in 1997 with the ex–Tony LaMasa *Ricky Nelson* '32 roadster, first place in 1999 with the former Dick Flint channeled '29-A, first place in 2001 with the So-Cal Speed Shop '34 competition coupe, and first place again in 2007 with the ex–Lloyd Bakan '32 3W.

The *Ricky Nelson* roadster, so-called because Ricky and his brother David drove it in a single appearance on the *Ozzie and Harriet* TV show, was purchased sight unseen. Complete and well preserved, it was far from Pebble Beach standards. Orosco had hoped to complete the Flint '29, but when that proved impossible, a few weeks prior to the 1997 show, he plunged into a major redo of the Ricky Nelson roadster. Despite a UPS strike that held up plating work, they reconstructed a section of the chassis, took the body down to bare metal, then re-plated, repainted, re-striped, and reupholstered the channeled roadster (trimmer Richard Santana did his work right in Orosco's shop) in just 17 days.

Orosco takes a cerebral approach to each restoration. With the Flint car, he was stymied by a bent and twisted Model A frame that had been modified repeatedly, crudely cut and re-welded, and severely weakened over time. Flint had been disappointed with the original work but didn't have the money at the time to redo it. He rationalized, "We didn't worry so much over things you didn't see."

"I had misgivings about the frame, and I agonized about what to do about it for five years." Orosco admits. With Dick Flint's blessing, Orosco's solution was to fabricate a new frame from a good original, replicating period hot rod construction techniques, right down to the rivets. "I tried to do what Dick would have done, if he could have taken the car to Frank Kurtis." Orosco kept the worn old chassis intact to show skeptics.

"*This* is what I would have done if I could've afforded it," Flint said, approvingly.

The restoration of the ex–Alex Xydias So-Cal Speed Shop '34 competition coupe was not without its challenges. The rare crankshaft-driven, 4-71 blower setup was unobtainable. Orosco's team made patterns and replicated it exactly. At the same time, they chased down hard-to-find parts like the Army Air

Corps surplus P-51 5-gallon de-icer tank adapted by Xydias for use as a fuel tank, as well as a float gauge for the water tank, originally used in a DC-3. Orosco's team showed the coupe at Pebble while wearing red and white Glendale Sidewinders Club jackets and period-style pith helmets. That doesn't count for points, but it's typical of Orosco's keen attention to detail.

If a particular part is needed for any of his projects, Orosco is relentless in his search. "I've been going to swap meets for 50 years. I love to find the 'you'll *never* find it' things. Maybe it's a childish motivation, but I love the hunt and where it takes me. I have a tremendous drive to find things now, place them in a car in a tasteful, period-correct manner, and share them with other people. I'm proud of my searching ability. Then I like to stand back proudly and watch people's reactions."

"I like things that are historic in nature," he continues. His first real hot rod was a '29 Model A Tudor, bought from a friend, fresh from competing at the '59 Oakland Roadster Show, running a 265-cid Chevy with three 2s. He later restored a MARC-winning '28 Model A Phaeton that took thirteen major awards, including a Best of Show where it out-pointed classic car entries from Bill Harrah and J. B. Nethercutt.

"I have a desire to get things absolutely right," he says, "the timeline, the color, the manufacturer's intent. And I've been vintage racing for 32 years, so I'm used to making parts or having them made for one-off cars. That's what we do. Historical accuracy is paramount, not chopping things up. With me, less is definitely more. The George Riley SOHC V-8-powered '32 roadster we just completed is geared toward those people who've really been there. The ultra-rare engine is one of just four examples. That car evokes strong emotions of where we came from, and I've never left. I'm rooted in old Fords. I have a deep appreciation for the past, but with subtle modifications.

"My guys can do *anything* I ask them to do. I was there, so my recollections, my magazine collection, my research helps me set goals and keep them on track. Some guys have a grand goal, but they lose their way. There might be several ways to do things. I want to do them the way we did 50 years ago.

"As a major developer," Orosco says, "I'm always under a magnifying glass, and I don't have any control over government rulings, zoning, etc. Doing my cars, there's no margin for error either, except it's with history. I'm always concerned about what people think. What we do is right out there for everyone to see. So I seek advice from people I respect; I ask questions, until I feel that I'm on track or off track. Olle [Ericksson] worked on the So-Cal coupe body, cutting out rusty sections and carefully welding in small panels for fifteen months to save as much of the original as possible. I could have gotten

> *Some guys have a grand goal, but they lose their way. There might be several ways to do things. I want to do them the way we did fifty years ago.*

a new steel body for that car, but it wouldn't have been right. I don't like excuses that begin with: 'Yes, but . . . '

"I replicate vintage components, like Bell Steering wheels and Eddie Meyer heads and manifolds, because we can do that," he says enthusiastically. "We've built entire Coventry-Climax engines; we reverse-engineered Ardun OHV heads. Here's the dichotomy: In my regular business, it takes so long to get feedback. A shopping center can take from four to ten years. But we can do those Veda Orr knock-off hubcaps or Elco twin-plug heads and go from idea to finished product in just six months. I satisfy a real creative need through the restoration process. It's so different from what I usually do in the course of a day. I pick and choose what we make, then sit back and enjoy the results like a proud parent. In contrast, here we are doing new development projects in Monterey and people tell us, 'We don't need any more construction. Why don't you go back to Fresno?'

"Reproducing the Ardun cylinder heads took a lot of money," he confesses. "People kept saying 'Speedy Bill Smith is going to do those,' so we had to be secretive, or I'd have lost a great deal. We did thirty complete sets, then I sold the patterns to Don Ferguson. He's done a great job with them. I sold out so I could finance another crazy project. My restorer side is evident here. We could have improved the rocker arm geometry on the Arduns, but that wasn't what we're about. We can do better metallurgy and CNC machining; we've got much better casting accuracy now. But I'm here as a visitor. I'm not comfortable modifying history.

"The way we price this stuff is important, too. If some guy spends forty years searching for genuine Smith heads, and I sell a reproduction set for a lot less money—that screws up the collectors. I try to be fair to everyone."

For all the great cars he's kept, Orosco has sold some important ones, including the ex–Jack Calori '36 Ford coupe, the chopped and channeled '40 Ford custom built by Valley Custom for Ralph Jilek, and the first Tom McMullen '32 roadster. "In the final analysis," he reasons, "if you restore one of these cars right (and that's the only way he'd do it), you can have a quarter of a million dollars in it. I'm more keenly interested in hot rods rather than customs. The McMullen car was a little too new for me. My timetable is 1948 to 1955. After that, when you start with blown Chevys and Buick nailheads, I'm finished. The Lloyd Bakan coupe is pushing it."

He sold the So-Cal coupe to Bruce Canepa. "I'd done everything I could with that car—Pebble Beach, the 'cacklefest,' etc., although sometimes," he confesses, "I'd really like to have it back. That said, its utility is so limited, and I like to drive my cars. If I ever retire, I want cars I can really use. We're doing a top and side curtains for the Riley roadster. You can tell he can't wait to get out on the road with that car—it's a rolling museum piece."

Orosco's shop completed a lovely '34 Ford 3W coupe last year in period Ford Tan. There's a polished SCoT-blown flathead under the hood, running a set of the late Barney Navarro's rare Hi-Dome heads. The interior is stock mohair, with a few rare gauges to spice things up. It flat takes your breath away. One of this car's neatest features is a period accessory horn that sounds like one on a Union Pacific diesel locomotive. Most people have never seen or heard anything like it. If Don Orosco knows where to find another one, he's not telling.

1932 FORD EX–LLOYD BAKAN THREE-WINDOW COUPE
owned by Don Orosco

1929 FORD EX–DICK
FLINT ROADSTER
owned by Don Orosco

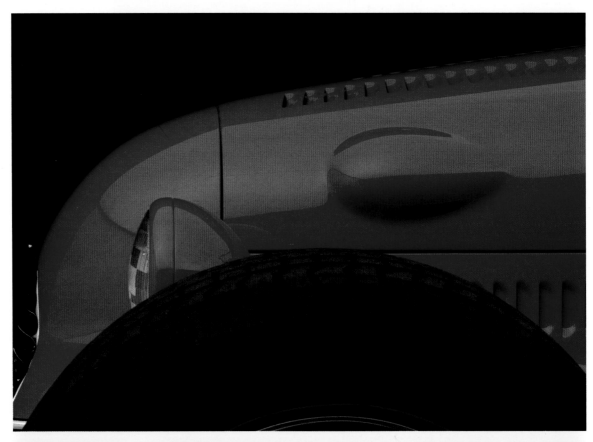

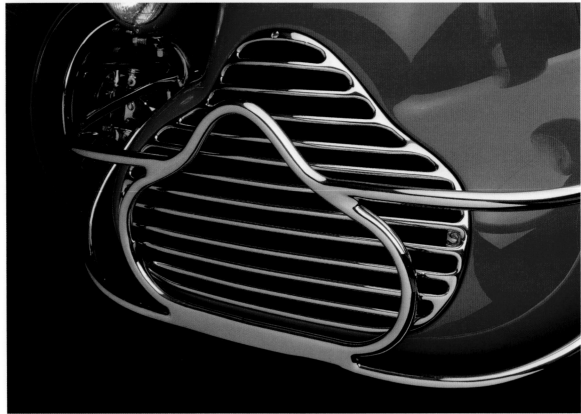

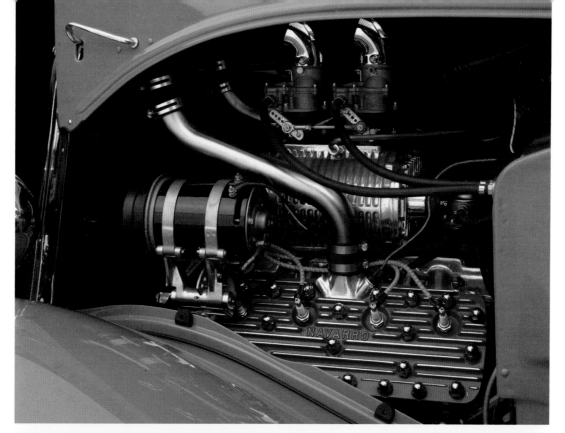

1934 FORD THREE-WINDOW COUPE owned by Don Orosco

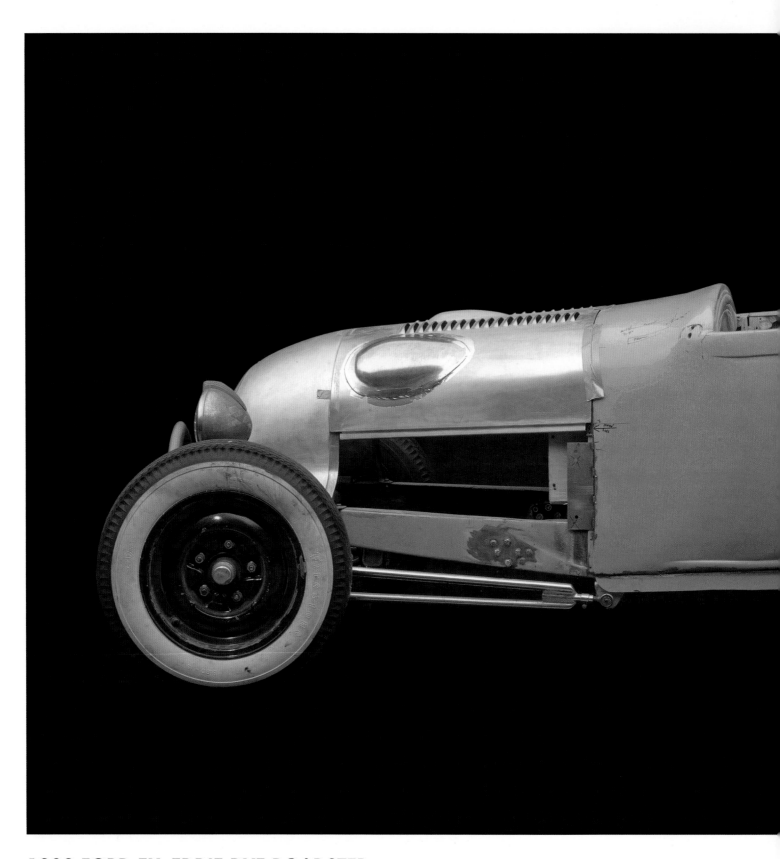

1929 FORD EX-EDDIE DYE ROADSTER owned by Don Orosco

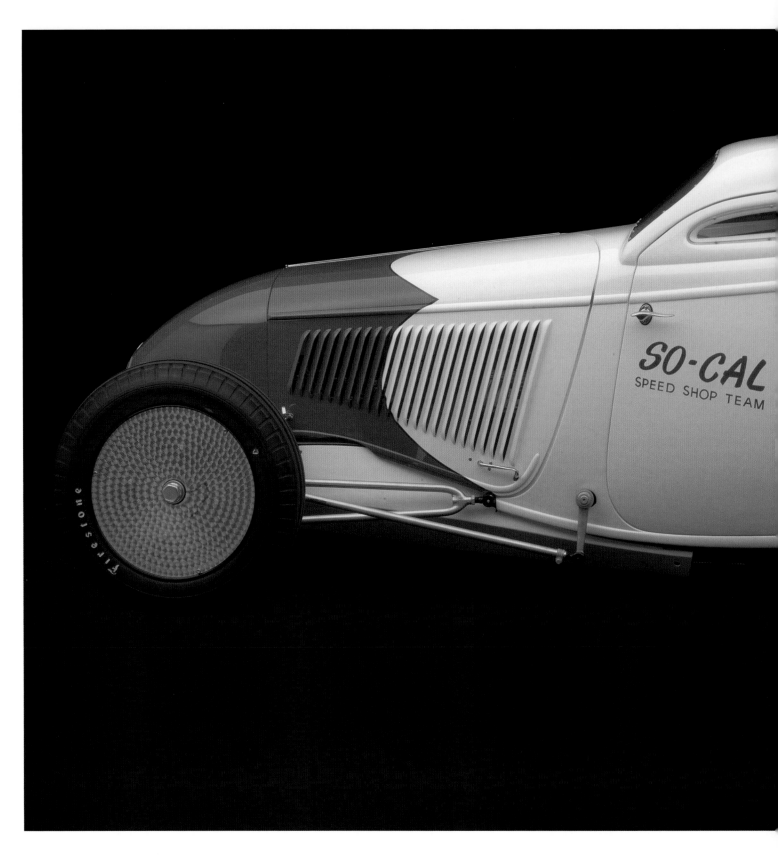

1934 FORD EX–SO-CAL THREE-WINDOW COUPE owned by Bruce Canepa

CHAPTER 14

RICHARD GRAVES
There's No Way Like the Old Way

His name might not be immediately recognizable to the average car show goer, and you'll probably never see him on TV, but for more than forty years, Richard Graves has been building special hot rods. Graves isn't known for design gimmicks or groundbreaking style. His cars aren't an amalgamation of rare parts, and they don't set speed records. Richard's Wheel and Chassis builds expertly engineered and meticulously assembled hot rods, with every bolt and weld reinforcing their reason for being: to be driven. That's all they do.

Graves, now 64, never strayed from the path he discovered very early on. A mechanic's son, he helped out in his dad's shop before he could "see the tops of the toolboxes." He says he'd reach up, feel around, and count over until he found the right socket. The day after high school ended, he took a job beside his father. In the mid-'60s, Graves started building hot rods out of his 1,000-square-foot home garage, moved into a dedicated shop in 1988, then into his current shop in 2000. He's never lived or worked anywhere but in Long Beach, California.

Early on, Graves discovered he had both the passion and aptitude for hot rodding. "My dad was just a mechanic. He didn't build anything, as far as custom stuff goes. I learned everything I did from doing it. Break something, do something wrong—I'd throw it in the trash and start over."

A trip around his shop tells you that not much is being thrown away these days. The assembly area is spotless, though a half-dozen cars are always in progress. The fabrication side of the shop has room for several chassis. Graves designs each one from the ground up. This section of the shop is surrounded by traditional machines of the rodding craft: English wheels, shrinker/stretchers, presses, welders . . . nothing here is computerized. It's all laid out just the way it was done in the early days. The back wall of the building hosts old cars, bodies, and parts-in-waiting stored high on a series of lifts and shelves. There's a complete 1932 Ford panel truck, a brace of Model A coupes, racks of flawless garnish moldings, and much more.

It's not uncommon to see so much vintage iron in one place, but it's comforting to know it will be treated with respect. If he had it his way, Richard might never build a high-dollar hot rod again. "I like beaters. That's what we called them way back. You'd find an old car with original paint and just buff it up and make a driver out of it. New hoses, new brakes, sure—then get out there and drive it. That's the kind of stuff I like to do. I like traditional '32s, '40s, the more stock-looking the better." This simple appreciation and respect for old cars runs so deep for Graves that he's never chopped the top on a car of his own.

At first glance, there seems to be little magic in his method. "Richard's rules" are a simple hot rod recipe. "One of the biggest things for me is wheels and tires. You've got to have them figured out before you start the job. You can't build a car and then try to find some wheels that fit on it. I'm crazy for steelies, stock hubcaps, and trim rings and all that. And I like older wheels, like Halibrands and Ansens." Graves is probably best known for a cool 1932 Ford Phaeton that was on the December 1972 *Rod & Custom* "Vintage Tin" cover. It's been named one of the 75 most significant Deuces ever. This was a pure driver, devoid of flash, a car that was sharply against the burgeoning trend to polished street rods.

Graves prefers original parts, like the majority of traditional builders, but this hard-and-fast rule is flexible if practicality mandates it. "I'm not fanatical about it," he says. "I use some reproduction stuff of course, but nothing fits like original parts. It's harder now to find stuff that's nice, so if you can buy a reproduction piece that'll work with a little adjustment, I feel it's better to buy it. You can buy a Brookville part, like a door, and I think you're better off to do that than to get an original door that'll need twenty to a hundred hours on it. I see nothing wrong with that."

It would be egregious to dismiss Graves as a simple reviver of relics. He's fully capable of delivering any of the endless variants of the hot rod genre. He followed his Phaeton with a sleek, smooth, Porsche-powered '33 Touring, though that experiment in the then-popular world of ultra-modern hot rods never won his heart. He has connections at Toyota, which has resulted in such technically impressive cars as a Lexus-powered '32 Ford highboy roadster and an early Toyota FJ45 (powered by a current Toyota NASCAR V-8) was chopped, channeled, and sectioned to resemble a traditional hot rod. When it's up to Richard, simple is best, and style is subordinate to substance.

Because his cars are so functional, they're very attractive. Think of the earliest hot rods that first fought timing clocks on dry lake beds—built for speed alone, these cars, and the purely technical reasons for their existence, were the genesis for today's traditional hot rodding trend. Richard's hot rods find that same allure in honest, pure mechanical perfection.

"My biggest thing is I'll wake up in the middle of the night thinking about how to build a certain part, in what order, not knowing what I want, but knowing you have to have this diameter first, then this taper." Graves is at his best when considering the minute mechanical problems of a car, and this is what's given him his edge. "I've finished a lot of cars that somebody else started. And that's where I learned about thinking ahead, because they'd built themselves into a corner, and I had to get them back out."

Graves credits the legendary Jim "Jake" Jacobs, a lifelong friend, and Ted Brown, one of the very first T-bucket builders and a man he worked beside for fifteen years, with helping him better understand the importance of engineering. Making a mechanical system perform better is the most basic tenet of hot rodding. Through endless trial and error, Graves has

perfected it. He smiles and says, "I've done a lot of things where you get it done and you don't like it, so you throw it away. A lot of things. I must like doing this, or else I wouldn't keep doing it."

He rarely plans a car out completely in advance. His hot rods are built from scratch, with he and his small but talented team doing all fabrication in-house, and the plans can change wildly as the build matures. For example, the shop recently finished a Model A coupe set apart by the rectangular openings of its '32 Chevrolet hood sides. This key idea came about in the final days of construction and was attempted on a whim.

> *One of the biggest things for me is wheels and tires. You've got to have them figured out before you start the job. You can't build a car and then try to find some wheels that fit on it.*

"The hood sides and top were all done," he says, "we just needed some louvers or something to cut up and put in there. They were something I hated for years, those '32 Chevy sides with the vertical 'doors.' I always thought they looked like crap. But as I got to thinking, I thought maybe if they were done right they wouldn't look that bad. I got some a week later, so we cut them out and put three of the doors in there, and it was done." With a lot of humility, Graves describes the process as, "It's not thinking too far ahead. I just kind of throw it together."

Combine his basic approach to style with a commitment to solid engineering and you get a sense for the no-frills attitude Graves espouses. It extends to his business and his feelings on modern car culture. "I've never been a car show type of guy," he says, which helps to explain why his name is a bit mysterious to the masses. "I'd rather just drive. I get more out of building the cars than I do out of shows." A client did have him build a cab-over-engine (COE) '38 Ford truck for the show circuit, and with Graves' touch, it took best in class at the Grand National Roadster

Show in Pomona. "I wouldn't have built the truck that way if I was building it for myself," he admits.

As far as client relations go, just because Graves can build *anything* doesn't mean he wants to. "The biggest thing I learned, and it took me a long time to learn it, was to say no. I used to do whatever they asked. Now, I tell them 'You need to take it somewhere else.'" If there is an aspect to modern rodding that bothers him, it's the sudden influx of would-be superstars with more money than knowledge. "There are guys that just want to buy into the system. They just don't understand what it takes to build a hot rod. You see them at a show, and they think they know everything about the hobby, but they couldn't put a car together if they had to."

Ever practical, Graves is critical of those builders who seem to revel in building sloppy, unsafe cars. "I don't mind if it's ugly, if they like doing that, but let's get some floorboards in there; let's have safe welds, safe fuel lines. A lot of guys will get a car done and the wipers won't work, the doors don't lock, there's no emergency brake, the throttle linkage is marginal, stuff like that. Little things that a lot of people just don't take the time to do." He jokes, "I'd no more ride in some of these cars than I'd try to fly."

After almost five decades, after more than 400 finished and driving cars, there is still real enthusiasm underneath Graves' quiet demeanor. As he walks you through his shop, pointing to framed photos and magazine covers of cars he's built, you can't help but share in his excitement. Graves creates hot rods with impeccable style, though in his mind, style hardly figures into it. His cars have impact like the first hot rods—the intrinsic appeal of early American cars made even better with exquisite craftsmanship and an intuitive grasp of automotive engineering. That's all there is to it, really. It's far more difficult than most can imagine, and Richard Graves makes it look easy.

1932 FORD PICKUP TRUCK owned by Richard Graves

1930 FORD MODEL A
FIVE-WINDOW COUPE
owned by Richard Graves

195X TOYOTA FJ40
owned by Toyota Motor Company

1939 FORD COE PICKUP
owned by Joe Gonzales

1934 FORD PHAETON
(POWERED BY PORSCHE)
owned by Richard Graves

CHAPTER 15

KENNEDY BROTHERS
Bombs Away!

In Pomona, California, if you know where to look, there's a shop with no sign. There's no sign because there's really no name. Those with graying hair remember it as "Early Iron." A decidedly younger set calls it the "Bomb Factory." Whatever you choose to call it, from behind the gate, among a smattering of surfboards, and beachcomber bikes, and accompanied by loud rock music, comes the work of brothers Joe and Jason Kennedy. Their honest, pull-no-punches approach to dedicated traditionalism has made them fast-rising stars in today's rodding world—a world they largely choose to ignore.

The brothers' facility could rightfully be thought of as the Kennedy family compound. Their father, Bob, a member of the Early Ford V8 Club, first used the space for restoring '33–'34 Fords. His shop, called Early Iron, was once a cluttered mix of independent metalworkers, fabricators, and engine builders, all of whom shared his small buildings (and fought over a single air compressor).

Joe and Jay began doing their own thing in the back, in what Joe describes as basically a "lean-to shack with a dirt floor."

"We weren't doing any fabrication," he says, "Jay was learning how to weld, so we just did paint and work other people didn't want. We were like 'Oh, we'll do it.'" In the early '90s, the elder Kennedy pushed everyone else out and passed the workspace on to his sons. But he didn't pass it on easily, cautioning his boys that there were more rewarding paths. "We were encouraged *not* to do it, since there's no money in it," Joe laughs, "which there isn't. It's the passion; that's why we're here. But you *can* make a living at it."

Today at the shop, the brothers' projects are balanced by a display case full of a lifetime's worth of model cars. Sixties muscle sleeps under racks of beach bikes and surfboards. Congratulatory postcards from celebrities and friends hang on the same wall as a pinup of Jane Mansfield and a mullet wig. These two might not take themselves too seriously, but don't be deceived; the passion Joe spoke of ties it all together.

The brothers are so focused on their work that they haven't taken the time to name their shop. "Bomb Factory" might be their best known handle, but even that was suggested by neighboring So-Cal Speed Shop after they offered to print some shirts—later realizing there wasn't anything to put *on* the shirts. "We don't really have any official name at all," Joe laughs. "Just whatever people call us. Kennedy Brothers, Bomb Factory; the shop was called Early Iron so people still call it that, so we got all sorts of aliases. Bomb Factory was So-Cal's deal, and it just stuck. So-Cal was selling the shirts, people were buying them actually—I couldn't believe it—so that's where it took off, that's where Bomb Factory came from. It's nothing we invented."

The brothers don't care, they are concerned only with their projects. Having moved away from the customs that dominated their early years ("They're all a bunch of Bondo'd up pieces of junk."), they took up what they had learned from their father: early Fords. They turned a corner in 2000 with their first serious 1932 Ford coupe. "It was really bad, just horrible," Joe says of the rusted pieces they started with. "It was just awful, but we built a nice show car out of it, and that kinda put us on the map."

What has come to separate the brothers from myriad other builders is a lack of pretense and a driving necessity to build honestly traditional cars. "You can open a *Hot Rod* magazine to November '63," Joe explains. "If you see it in the magazine, or saw it on the streets back then, okay, that's how this car would have looked. We really try to focus, when we build a car, to fit a very certain specific time. You want something to emulate what this car would have looked like . . . like if I'd have seen that car in Bellflower what it would have looked like."

Also separating the pair, and endearing them even further to today's ever-youthful traditionalists, is that they speak their minds without hesitation."I laugh at cars that have all sorts of mixed shit on them," says Joe. "They have all the best of everything, and that's fine, but it's not really a period car, it's just a modern version of an old car . . . it's a conglomeration. Everything we do was already done way back when. There's nobody really breaking any new ground. What we're into is repeat radio. It's the same old stuff over and over. We're influenced by that old stuff, not really anything that's modern day."

Highlighting this philosophy is what Joe considers his favorite car. Even if the Kennedy brothers' cars sell for amounts approaching six figures, the one that brings the biggest smile to his face is a beater. "One of my personal favorites was a jalopy '34 Ford two-door sedan. Jim Jard owns it now. We were into roundy-round cars, racecars, so we made it a jalopy car you would have seen here on the West Coast. It was streetable, so we had to deviate in a few spots here and there, but that car was fun. We just threw it together from a bunch of rusty bodies that were junk. You can get in it, drive it, beat it up, don't have to worry about scratching the paint . . . people get excited when they see it."

Next on the list is that first '32 five-window. "That was gratifying just because it started as such a horrible pile of shit. It was made from a couple of bodies, and we built a nice car-show car out of it, with black, smooth, flawless bodywork."

Here, again, is where the brothers deviate from the accepted norms. They might have broken out with a "car show" car, but they'll never seek the spotlight. "No, no competition," Joe says. "I don't want to compete with a bunch of clowns. That's it, period. Everybody's got their ego out there; we're not ego people or anything. I don't mind, I like car shows, and I'll take stuff to show people, but as for competition, it's just a bunch of babies. It's not our scene."

Their scene deviates strongly from rodding's ruling class, that of the million-dollar roadsters and the concept-driven art projects. They dress like surfers, talk like surfers, and they are approachable and friendly—but only so far as you're on their side. And the Kennedy brothers like stirring the pot. Theirs is still the land of dropped axles, original paint, chromed wheels (chromed reverse rims are okay, too, provided the car comes from a late-enough time period), and hot flatheads and early small-blocks. And they work to keep it that way, selecting their clients carefully.

"You gotta be selective, you don't want to get burned by anybody," Joe claims. "We're not big-time . . . we're busy." Too much of today's rodding culture, he feels, draws too heavily from the *perceived status* of hot rod ownership, not the genuine appreciation for the cars. "There's some people that are just in it because their friends are into it, and *their* friends are into it, and

> *What we're into is repeat radio. It's the same old stuff over and over. We're influenced by that old stuff, not really anything that's modern day.*

their friends are, and they don't have any reason why. They might be into it for a couple of years, and next thing you know they're out Frisbee golfing somewhere, they're out following *that* dream."

High-dollar rodders represent an even larger problem to Joe. "The generations are changing. People can't afford it, and their interest isn't there. Nobody can even relate to that older shit anymore. They're not like, 'Oh I can't wait to have some money in the bank to go get one of those Model Ts and drive it around.' It'll be the same with a lot of this stuff, newer people aren't gonna relate to it. It's sad to say. It's changing in front of us right now. The supply of parts is dried up; people that have the stuff won't relinquish it. And besides, it's too expensive, so people are gonna go do other alternatives . . . it's just my opinion, not the truth, just my opinion."

Right now the two are restoring a '50s-era fuel dragster, with its original nitro-burning flathead and Kent Fuller chassis, and they'll be happy to take it

north to Bakersfield for the Hot Rod Reunion's legendary annual Cacklefest. But they have an ulterior motive. "It'd be fun to take it to the Cacklefest, be a bunch of bums, and everybody'll say, 'Where'd these guys get this car; who did that?' Well it's our car; we own it. You got all those high-rollers there that own all those cars; it's just like the car shows. It's a big stroke-off for everyone's ego. We're on a budget, we don't have much money, but to have a pretty badass car to take and shove it in their face, it's gonna be great to say 'Look what we did.'"

Joe says this with a huge grin on his face. But the brothers certainly take themselves and their work seriously, spending all day, every day, in the open air of their original parts-cluttered workspace. "We're just having fun. We're having a good time. We totally enjoy what we do. We love building cars. We never set out to make a dent in society or anything. If people like our stuff, that's great. We appreciate the fanfare. We're just average people following our dreams and building nice, quality cars. I consider us more artists than anything else. Just doing our art. People like it, so it's cool. If we die like Picasso, Van Gogh, or whatever, die like they did, on the street, poor, well, maybe we'll die like that.

"We're just doing our own thing," Joe says. "You got dreams? Chase 'em. I know it doesn't happen to everybody. We were pretty fortunate, being here, growing up here, having a place to work . . . and our Dad helped us out a lot. He was kind of against us doing this, but he got us our start, so I gotta give our old man a lot of credit for getting us where we're at right now.

"But don't listen to *your* parents."

1941 MERCURY COUPE
owned by Lynn Williams

1936 FORD ROADSTER
owned by Lynn Williams

1932 FORD FIVE-WINDOW COUPE *DEVIL DEUCE* owned by Jim Jard

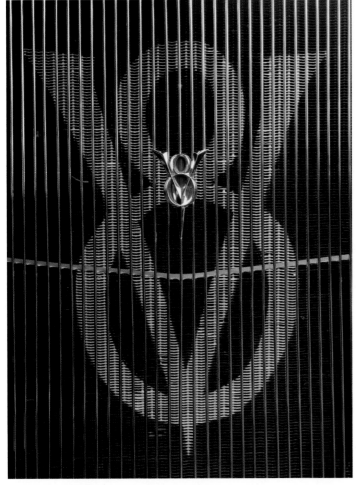

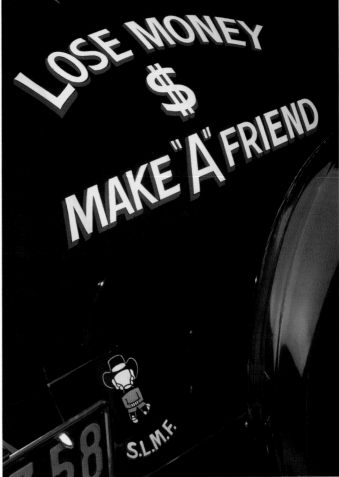

1933 FORD ROADSTER owned by Lynn Williams

1932 FORD
THREE-WINDOW COUPE
EX–KENNEDY BROTHERS
owned by Steve Giosso

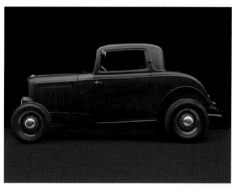

CHAPTER 16

PETE CHAPOURIS
This Changes Everything

In five decades of hot rodding, Pete Chapouris has shifted the entire hobby on its axis a handful of times. His first business brought quality, mass-produced aftermarket parts to do-it-yourselfers everywhere. He revived the idea of coupes as "real" hot rods. A decade later Chapouris was on the cutting edge of the fat-fendered movement, and with some amazing restorations in the '90s he firmly entrenched the idea of preserving classic hot rods. Today he's the standard bearer of the legendary So-Cal Speed Shop name, guiding the shop forward with a careful balance of artistic creativity and business acumen.

Like so many other second-generation rodders (Chapouris was born in 1942), his expertise stems from a rare combination of mechanical skill, an artistic eye, and an unabridged passion for cars. Chapouris grew up prepared to spend his years much as his father did, at Los Angeles–area dynamometer manufacturer, Clayton Industries. Instead he soon felt an irresistible urge to leave. "I think the reason I wanted to go out on my own was I had this pent-up ambition to build cars. I thought I had the artistic ability and the know-how to do it. I can remember making brackets and looking at them and thinking there's a space for me out there, *doing* something." Hot rodding was his calling. "Making parts for hot rods was a natural for me. I can't remember not *ever* being turned on by cars. I wish I can play guitar like Billy Gibbons can," he says of the ZZTop musician, longtime friend, and frequent So-Cal customer. "But I can't do that, and he can't weld, so . . . "

Chapouris has been on a winning streak ever since. His chopped, flamed '34 Ford three-window, *The California Kid*, paired with Jake Jacobs' yellow '34 on the cover of the November 1973 *Rod & Custom*, made enough waves that the two founded Pete & Jake's the next year. Still around under different ownership, this company was one of the first to bring well-engineered, quality suspension parts into home garages nationwide. In the '90s his eponymous PC3G enterprise impeccably restored the Doane Spencer '32 roadster and the Pierson Brothers '34 coupe, ensuring that important hot rods would be reborn rather than recycled.

Today he runs the resurrected So-Cal Speed Shop, flying a flag originally raised by Alex Xydias in 1946. It's now an enormous nationwide operation with 10 retail stores and a thriving mail-order parts and clothing division. Most meaningful to Chapouris is what it *means* to be So-Cal. After meeting the legendary Xydias and, in fact, securing the rights to the name, his entire perspective changed. "I thought, 'I could screw up this guy's reputation overnight!' It became a legacy. I really feel it. I feel that it's real important for that name to carry on. So I'm real strict about it. I don't want anybody going in there and ripping off anything that belongs to Alex, or anything that he's worked on for the last 62 years. I protect it. I feel really obligated to it, and to his family . . . my dad died in '85, and Alex and I got together and did this in '97. He's kind of been my dad since then."

Chapouris hasn't just carried on the So-Cal name, he's enhanced it. He describes the shop's work as, "eclectic as hell." So-Cal crafts everything from beautifully built street rods, dead-nuts accurate restorations, and artfully customized imports, to record-setting land speed racers. "I don't want this to come off sounding self-centered or strange," he explains, "but if I have a talent, if there's any genius in any of this, it's being able to visualize just about anything *finished*. I look at *all* modified cars as hot rods. It doesn't matter what they are. I've always had a hot rod, and I've always had a custom. I like both early and late models. I think that's where we stand above a lot of other shops. Everything's different. I don't like to do the same thing twice."

Chapouris is the man behind the curtain. He oversees the design of every car, deals with clients directly, and ensures his staff functions as a team. "I do all the design work. Everything we start with is mine. I work with three excellent artists: Thom Taylor, Chris Frogget, and Alberto Hernandez. All three of us have this wire between us. I can literally talk with them over the telephone about what I want to do, and they will give me that exactly. Then we'll talk to the client and make sure that he's happy. We might make a few changes, but I set the parameters. I can see it done, I can see us driving it, the whole nine yards."

Chapouris often compares himself to a movie producer or a band leader in his dual roles as designer and businessman—he might lead, but others now do the hard work. "Bottom line is, it's about the guys that build the car. It's not about me. I like that camaraderie of getting together with people and sharing ideas because we all come up with original thoughts, and a lot of the stuff I've come up with is changed under the influence of the people I was around."

This philosophy doesn't only serve Chapouris, or the shop, but the team members themselves. Ace So-Cal fabricator Jimmy Shine is a hot rod celebrity in his own right, and current shop foreman Ryan Reed is establishing himself as a top-flight craftsman—yet both are years away from gray hair. "When they leave here they've got to have a reputation. They have to take it with them to stay in the industry."

This is necessary, he feels, to guarantee the future of hot rodding. "I wear my industry hat a lot. I'm constantly looking for better things for the industry. Do the best you can with the cars you're building, and grow the industry," he commands. "There's plenty of room for everybody. I don't consider *anyone* competition. I consider them all partners." His concern and selflessness earned him a spot in the SEMA Hall of Fame in 1999.

Chapouris easily handles the usual rocky relationships with clients, thanks to the good will he and his crew have built up. "As a builder, and I think there's not a builder in the country that would disagree with me, the hardest thing to do is to guess what a car's gonna cost, try to keep it on a budget, and keep the customer happy. It's really, really difficult. Work is always over budget, and clients are always upset. It works out in the end because the guy gets a quality piece. If we do one thing badly, it's estimating time. If we do one thing well, it's building really bitchin' stuff. I tell every client the same thing: when we're done with this car you won't be embarrassed. You won't make excuses for it. You can just stand next to it and let people drool all over it."

The unifying factor in all of this is Chapouris' unabashed, unyielding love for rodding and customizing. It comes out in waves when he's pressed to pick a favorite out of his hundreds of projects. "It's

> ❝ *If I have a talent, if there's any genius in any of this, it's being able to visualize just about anything finished. I look at all modified cars as hot rods. It doesn't matter what they are.* ❞

hard to say because they all become like children. I think the car that I probably had more fun in was my purple '39. It was a drag car, it was a great road car, it was a good mountain car, it was fast, and I think it was a bit ahead of its time because the fat-fendered thing hadn't really taken off yet. *Limefire* (his top-75 Deuce-winning '32 roadster) was a lot of fun, but it was on the ragged edge of being too much car. That thing was a real racecar. I think about *The California Kid*. A lot of times you say you're never gonna out-do *that* car. I never wanted a car more than I wanted that coupe. I was possessed—young and possessed. I don't ever remember lusting over a car as much as I did that one. And I had fun in my

'50 Chevy hardtop. And my dad's car brings back great memories. If I could choose one car to drive back and forth to work it'd probably be the '39. But if I could add it to my collection, it would be very hard not to say *California Kid's* the one."

Artist, team leader, businessman, and industry spokesman: they all revolve around Chapouris' passion. "I've got these memories of when I was a kid, of seeing cars, on special days, like I'm walking home from school and there's this buddy of mine that had a chopped five-window, and it was red primer, and it had chromed Merc wheels and whitewalls on it, a hood top but no sides, a flathead, white tuck and roll in it, and he had chrome plated all the window frames. It was really nice inside. His girlfriend, a dynamite little blonde, was driving this car, and the sun was just dancing off the inside of it. I'll never forget that sight as long as I live."

Pete often brings memories like that one to life. "One of the things that I do that I think keeps the crew going here is we'll finish a car, like J. J. Barnhardt's gold five-window, and there's no 'I' or 'me' in there, it's 'us.' I don't even care about being mentioned in the article. The guys built the car. I conceived it, I hatched it, I saw the car finished, I got the color, I knew exactly what I wanted out of it. Luckily, J. J.'s the kind of guy who trusts me completely, I mean right down to the width of the tuck and roll and where the tinted glass and the chrome belongs.

"I want other people to feel the same way about their cars as I feel about the cars that I build. I can remember *The California Kid*; I'd worked on that car by myself one night over at the old Pete & Jake's in Temple City, and about half the car was sticking out of the garage. The outside light was on it. I wasn't thinking about anything, but I looked up and the car startled me. It turned me on as much right then, 14 years later, as it did the very first time I drove it. *That's* what drives me. I want to have other people feel the same way about *their* stuff. I don't think I have anything left to prove except that I love doing this. That's really all it is."

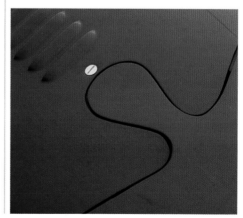

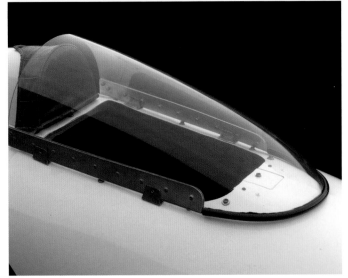

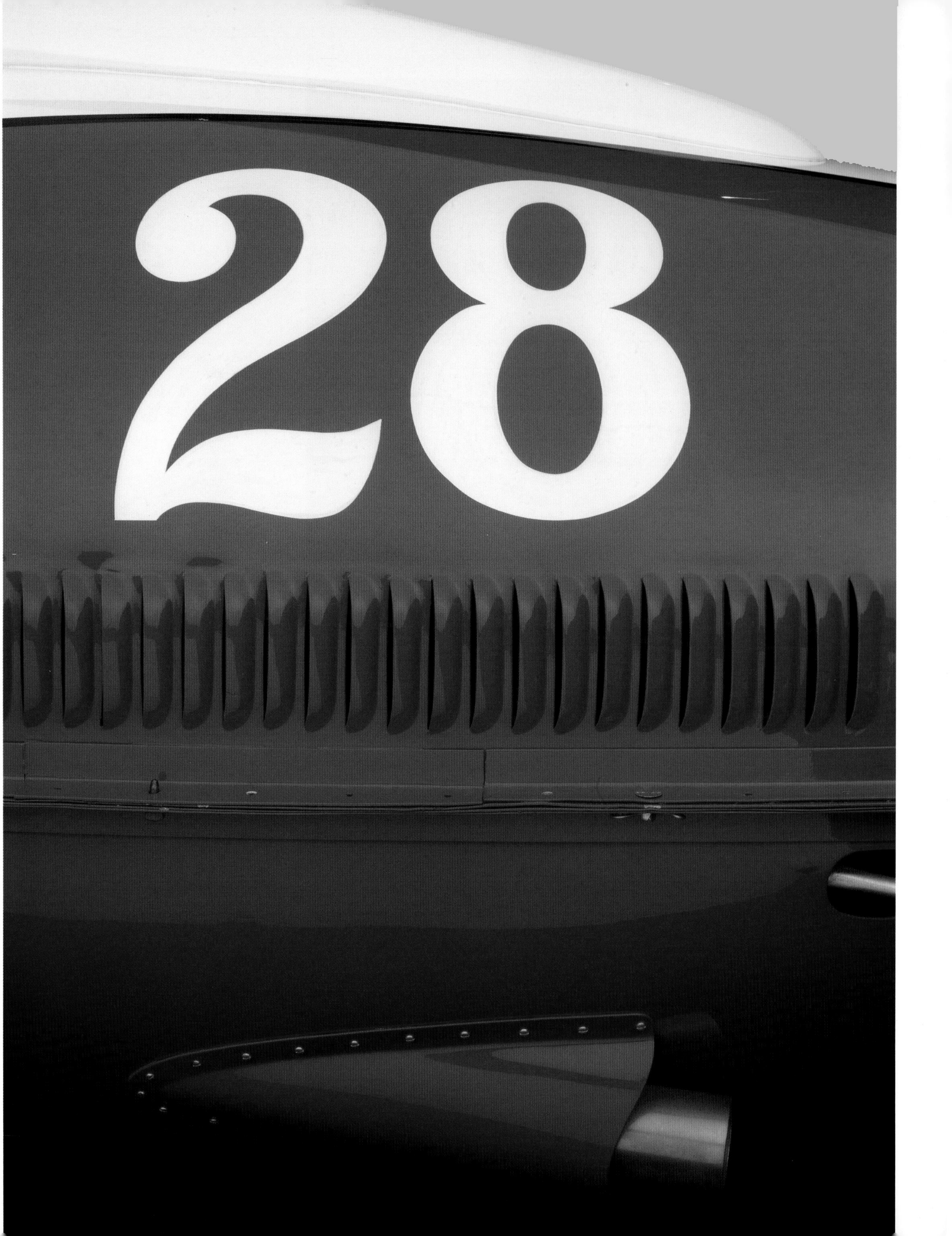
28

1935 FORD PICKUP TRUCK ('34 GRILLE)

owned by Billy Gibbons

1966 CHEVROLET CHEVELLE HARDTOP

owned by Billy Gibbons

1932 FORD ROADSTER
EX–DOANE SPENCER
owned by Bruce Meyer

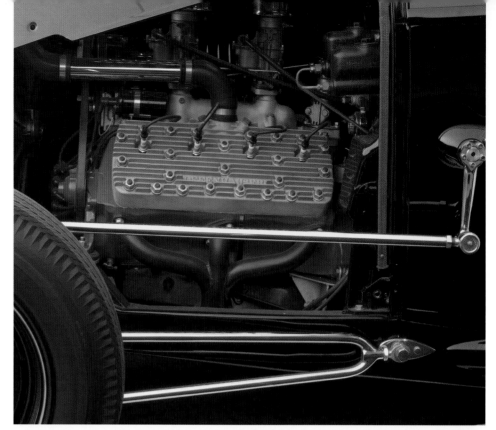

1934 FORD ROADSTER owned by Todd and David Haas

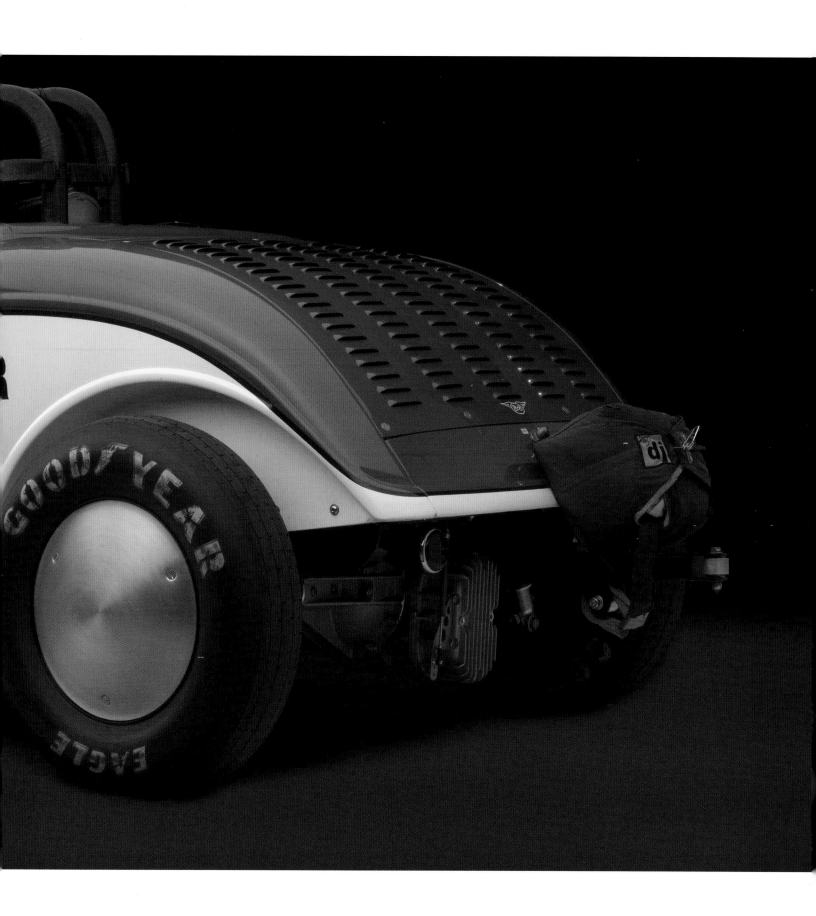

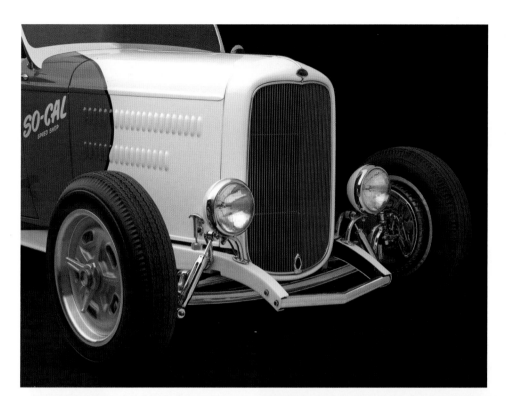

1932 FORD ROADSTER
owned by Pete Chapouris

CHAPTER 17

ZANE CULLEN
Youth Will Be Served

Less than a mile off the freeway, almost hidden in the back of a nondescript Santa Rosa, California, business park, you'll find Zane Cullen. His shop mirrors the town. It's deceptively quiet and meticulously clean. But swirling black marks on the parking surface shatter any pretense that Cullen's cars mirror his laid-back surroundings.

Born in the early '70s, Cullen missed the first generations of hot rodding, depending on where you draw the lines. Unlike many current young builders, whose appreciation of early hot rodding is evidenced by copious body art, pseudo-'40s dress, and loud rockabilly music, Cullen's lack of tattoos, pressed denim, and "movie star" hair makes it clear his focus is strictly on the cars. He blends a thorough understanding of artistic design, an unwavering standard of craftsmanship, and a profound knowledge of vintage and contemporary automotive performance, both European and American.

Cullen's hot rods are not like those of a traditional hot rod shop. They're artistic creations. While drawing inspiration from the past, Cullen hopes his cars "transcend the inherent limitations of many early hot rods. In styling terms, they were sometimes awkward-looking cars that emphasized total function before form. But there were always elements that were awe-inspiring."

He's intrigued by the daredevil nature of early racing. "Those guys were fearless," he exclaims. "Then builders like [Harry] Miller came along and beautified everything from the engine to the outside aesthetics. The factory craftsmen *engine-turned* the blocks on some Bugattis! I really admire that type of craftsmanship," he confesses. "I want to integrate style and speed into one."

Assimilating pre-war Indy-, dirt-, and board-track racing with early hot rodding *and* traditional European motorsports would be a monumental task for any builder, let alone a relative youngster from Northern California who didn't exactly grow up surrounded by these classics. "My dad was not a hot rodder, but he loved old cars, so there were always magazines around like *Cars and Parts*. I was exposed to a variety of cars. Maybe at an early age I saw some early Ferraris or Aston Martin racecars and thought they were neat? There are so many little micro-cultures in the automotive world that anytime you find out about one you don't know, it's intriguing. I guess it's just what I was destined to do. When I look back, I was always passionate about cars."

Passion can be an overused term, but Cullen epitomizes it. He relates how as a young boy he displayed savant-like skill at naming cars, calling out makes and models by the shape of their headlights at night. (He calls it a Rainman skill, and it's still with him. Drive around with Cullen and point out an ugly modern SUV. He can tell you the make, model, designer, and influence from about a thousand feet away.) As a kid, when Cullen was punished and sent to his room, he wouldn't just read *Hot Rod* and other magazines, he'd lay a dozen on the floor and play the, "I'd have done it this way" game. More enthusiastic about the artistic side of cars than the engineering side, by his early teens Cullen wanted to be an automotive designer.

"I wanted to go to Art Center in Pasadena," he says, referring to the Transportation Design program at the Art Center College of Design. Recent graduates include hot rod photographer David Perry and one of the biggest names in popular hot rodding today, Chip Foose. While attending junior college and preparing academically for Art Center, Cullen "started hearing horror stories" about the life of an OEM designer. "You graduate and you go to work for somebody designing door handles, or wheels, and when you're 50 you start designing a whole car. Maybe it's not that way now, but *that* really freaked me out."

Already plying his custom craft, Cullen picked up the painter's trade at his father's auto body shop. Another shop took Cullen under its wing when he was 16. He started at the bottom, cleaning up and sanding. One day the shop's painter quit. "So I had to paint a Studebaker; that's just how it worked. By the time I was 19, I was responsible for everything from bodywork forward, and there were only three of us there. The owner would do the metalwork and rub out the Bondo, then give it to me. I'd finish it, paint it, rub it, and give all the pieces to the third guy for assembly."

At the same time Cullen was building a hopped-up Volkswagen—all the rage in Northern California at the time—for his girlfriend (today she's his wife). A local guy saw his workmanship and asked for his input on the paint for his '36 Ford roadster project. Cullen saw it and offered his services. As he was finishing up, the benefactor showed up with "a '40 Ford convertible that was in two halves. He asked me if I wanted to keep working, so I said 'Yeah, pay me by the hour!'" Cullen finished that project, then others, then some for the benefactor's friends, and eventually, in 1993, it was time to open his own place. With a business partner, Creative Concepts was born.

Cullen's work has evolved from finishing others' projects and taking whatever work was available to "designing" radical hot rods of his own. Which leads to two important points. First, for Cullen, he's not designing these cars. "I hate to call it designing," he says. Even if you graft a boattail rear to a '32 Ford, it's still a '32 Ford. "To me, it's restyling. Much of what we do has already been done. You can put a spin on it, but true designers really move emotion and take it to another level." That simple ethos is why his work has such appeal. Cullen's respect for tradition,

for history, and for the racecars from the first half of the last century prevents him from destroying their classic lines. He incorporates cues from all over the automotive map when he's crafting a car.

Some critics feel he can be too free with his associations, that maybe Aston Martins and Muroc never crossed paths for a reason. This leads into a second important point about Cullen's work. It's another set of choices that sometimes distances ultra-traditionalists from his cars. Specifically, his boattail Deuce resembles a beautiful remnant from the early '20s heyday of board-track racing, where Millers and Duesenbergs competed at speeds up to 140 mph—until you get to the engine. It's a four-banger, like a dirt- or board-track racer would have run, but this is a 21st century Ford/Mazda PZEV 2.3-liter 4-cylinder. His reasoning is clear and convincing.

> ❝ *Most roadsters today have lost the essence of what made those original cars great. They were stripped-down racers; they were pushing the envelope.* ❞

"Whether it's the speedster or a '61 Corvette, I try to improve on the original design. And I like integrating new technology. Most roadsters today have lost the essence of what made those original cars great. They were stripped-down racers; they were pushing the envelope. That raw, natural aesthetic of original hot rodding really appeals to me."

He praises Jon Hall and Mark Kirby, two well-known Detroit-area rodders who have pushed the bar with Hall's larger-dimensioned '27 Ford roadster body and Kirby's all-new aluminum flathead engine. "Their predecessors," Cullen explains, "guys like Navarro, Isky, all the greats, that's what they did." It's a parallel that goes all the way back to Harry Miller, who not only created his own engines but developed the very alloys from which they were formed. "That kind of thinking is inspiring," Cullen says.

Creative Concepts took the 2003 Builder of the Year award at the Grand National Roadster Show in San Mateo. In 2004, Goodguys presented Cullen with its Trendsetter award. Equally inspirational was the in-person appreciation Cullen experienced when his *Deuce Speedster* debuted at the San Francisco Rod, Custom, and Motorcycle Show. "We were in the Arena section, next to builders like Brizio and D'Agostino. Guys from the 'Suede Palace' were saying it was their favorite car. A world-renowned tattoo artist said it was the best car in the show, and an old guy who used to race Offy midgets said the same thing. Chip [Foose] wanted to trade me one of his cars for it. Winning over several noted builders showed me I did my job. When you can accomplish something like that, it's pretty rare."

Summing up his influences, Cullen says, "There's a lot of different elements, whether it's early road racing or early Formula One stuff or early dry lakes cars. When you look at all those different avenues, all those early aspects created their own style, but it happened accidentally, over time. But *that's* what starts tradition."

Synthesizing and distilling disparate traditional elements while embracing modern performance, Cullen bought out his partner, Dennis Hartwig, and dropped Creative Concepts as the name of the shop. Santa Rosa is eight miles from Cotati, an area steeped in automotive tradition. From the board-track speedway that existed from 1921–22, to drag racing in the '50s and '60s at Cotati Drag Strip, and world-class road racing at Cotati Raceway from 1957 to 1972, Cotati was prominent in motorsports of all kinds.

After meeting with local old-timers, collecting information and photography, and obtaining the local racers' blessings, Cullen wants to do for the area what he's done with hot rods. Under the umbrella of automotive performance, he's gathered differing quests for speed together in one place. Look for Cullen at the Cotati Speed Shop. And don't expect to see anything resembling the status quo.

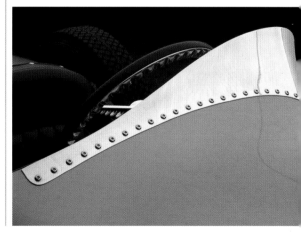

1933 FORD *SPEEDSTAR* CHASSIS
owned by Ed and Kendra Knudson

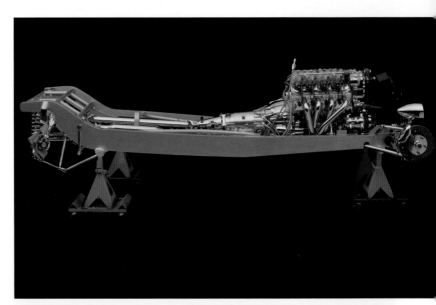

1932 FORD ROADSTER
owned by Mike and Kelly Winrod

1932 FORD ROADSTER owned by Darin and Michelle Tunstall

1940 WILLYS WOODIE owned by Richard and Cindy Long

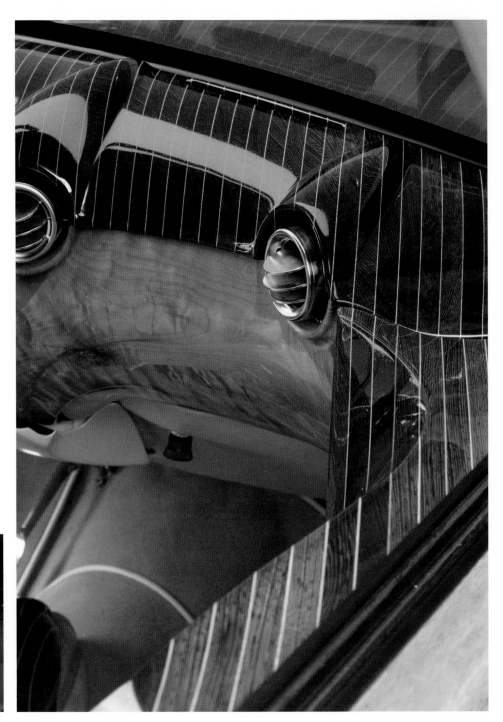

Steve Moal's 10,000-square-foot shop in Oakland, California, is known for superb metal fabrication. "It's a family business that dates back to 1946 with my grandfather," Moal says. "I started doing body and fender work and customizing cars right out of high school. It was the natural thing for me to do. In 1971, when I took over, we were primarily a collision shop for Mercedes-Benz and high-end makes. We did restoration and specialty bodywork on Ferraris and classics. The demand for expert metalwork grew and grew in the '80s and '90s. Now, that's all we do."

A stone hot rodder himself, Steve's personal '32 Ford was featured in *Street Rodder* magazine in 1981. Later, he was "heavily involved with Tom Walsh's '34 tub (an *HR* magazine cover car). We did all the metalwork, right down to fabricating the hinges." Steve's novel California V-8 speedster, a racecar-inspired T with an Italian accent, helped him win the Oakland Roadster Show Builder of the Year title in 1995. "Tim Allen saw that car," says Steve. "He wanted to buy it, or have me build one for him. The result was a roadster Allen called *The Licorice Stick.*"

Moal's most publicized works have been bespoke efforts for Eric Zausner, an imaginative San Francisco businessman who's also a serious car and motorized miniature model (spindizzie) collector. "We started doing small jobs for Eric on vintage Ferraris. He watched us complete the two speedsters. Then we built him an even wilder car—a brilliant styling amalgam called the *Torpedo.* The grille is pure Alfa 8C2900." A Ferrari Barchetta Touring's bold beltline reveal became the new car's visual focal point. The rich finish is classic Alfa, a dark red hue that first appeared on the P2/P3 Scuderia Ferrari racers of Tazio Nuvolari and Achille Varzi, and later on postwar Ferraris. Classic hot rod styling elements were skillfully applied, like the split windscreen, a DuVall reincarnate, and the *Torpedo*'s purposeful, Deuce-roadster-like stance. The stunning mix proves how well this Franco-American collaboration succeeded. As Eric describes it, "I wanted to see what would happen if an Italian guy built a hot rod out of pre- and postwar Italian car parts."

That conceptual approach has since been repeated by Zausner and Moal, with a '32 Ford roadster imaginatively "built by an Indy mechanic in the 1940s" fronted by a Miller-style grille, incorporating the best speed parts of that era. They followed that with a boattail speedster that morphed Auburn, Ford, and Duesenberg elements into a stunning black stiletto of a car. Keeping its hand in, Moal's shop restored the Eddie "Rochester" Anderson Special for Zausner, a car once owned by the famous black comedian who played Jack Benny's valet for many years on syndicated radio shows.

Working with sons David (production manager) and Michael (design and engineering) and his wife Teresa (business manager), Steve and his team do nearly everything in-house: concept work, fabrication, chassis construction to racecar standards—often with sophisticated pushrod suspension—and perfect paint. Ken Nemanic in Walnut Creek does the shop's trimming.

"We make most bodies ourselves," adds Moal. "I prefer to build from scratch. That's where you're challenged to be the most creative. And with that challenge, you have a responsibility. There's always a chance, a risk, that you might build an ugly car. When people trust you to build a car, they want it to be beautiful. That's what cranks me on the most, to scratch-build something that's stunning."

Moal has an even, measured temperament that helps him work well with even the most powerful and demanding clients. "With Eric Zausner's Barchetta," Steve notes, "he wanted it to be very Italian, inspired by all things Italian. That was his dream, and we discovered the shape and design of that car together. Our clients all come to us for a reason; they saw something we built that they liked. Then they want us to build *their* dream car."

Moal's shop combines traditional fabrication techniques, like forming panels on an English wheel, with building scale models in clay and foam, doing full-sized drawings, and even creating CAD drawings in 3D. "One thing that gives us a great edge," he confides, "as a result of restoring old Italian cars, is that we get to look over the shoulders of those builders and see how they did it. We *know* how it was done.

"We understand the way these guys made things," he emphasizes, "like the *superleggerra* system of building a lightweight tubular framework. When you know that, you start to get the feeling of what a design really ought to be. The cockpit needs to be a certain size for two people, the wheelbase and track need to be within reason, then the formula isn't that difficult. Our cars don't look alike. We wanted to recapture the feeling of an early Alfa, to preserve all those influences. Eric's car could have been a hot rod built in Italy, with its Carrello headlights, Brembo brakes, Maserati taillights, other Italian parts—all those bits we made had to be influenced by Italian practice.

"It doesn't matter if we're doing a racecar, an Indycar, a lakes roadster, a Bonneville or dry lakes racer, you've got to have some sort of a baseline. You have to be pretty clear on a concept to begin with," he emphasizes. "Otherwise you wander off course. I don't think that Alfa grille shell of Eric's would look good on a real '32 Ford."

After 30-plus years of building memorable cars, what's changed? "Everything's changing and it's going to continue to change," he answers, "but it will be as interesting as ever it was. The materials, the methods in which we make things like computer-aided milling machines and laser jets, that's all changed. And yet we still beat panels; we've kept

those skills. That's still a very cost-effective way to make a one-off. If you want something that's unique, and it's made of metal, making it by hand is still the best way.

"Today, we have assistance from computers with electronic motor management; *that's* a big change." For the 456 V-12 Ferrari, those electronics were a challenge. We can get the mechanical parts in the car and mechanically lash the thing up, that's not the problem. But can we make it start, idle, and perform? It's not a simple matter. Some companies, like Robert Bosch, won't share technical information. So it becomes a pretty tricky deal.

> ❝ *I prefer to build from scratch. That's where you're challenged to be the most creative. And with that challenge, you have a responsibility. There's always a chance, a risk, that you might build an ugly car.* ❞

"I look back for my own experience, but you don't always want to do *that* again; that's the way it's always going to be for creative people. To me, a hot rod is a lightweight, '30s-era, vintage car with a very powerful engine. I still consider old Fords as hot rods. But it's changing every day. Our 'lowbelly' tubular chassis is really a contemporary hot rod—but it's a new twist on that old formula. We know how to make independent suspension, but we specifically didn't do that because I still see a beam axle in a hot rod. I love '32 grille shells; it's hard to improve on that design.

"Much of what we do is a blend of old and new," he muses. "The newest car on the circuit, at auto shows like Paris and Geneva, is going to be a blend of the designers' experiences. Most people are getting the same vibes. In the '50's, cars with fins were inspired by jet aircraft. That's why there are trends; we're all inspired by the same things.

"I admire great fabrication," Moal says, and you sense this job has not lost its fascination for him. "Just go to Paris and see the metalwork, the beam sections, etc. Great design is everywhere in our lives. I look at that a lot; I'm inspired by that stuff. And I'm constantly looking away from automobiles because that's how you come up with something that's unique, or a new way of packaging it."

Does he like the work of other builders? "That's a tough call; they're close personal friends. I love everything Roy Brizio does because we're such friends. But builders that didn't do hot rods inspire me, too, like Scaglietti and Touring. And I'm friends with [motorcycle builders] Bob Dron and Arlen Ness; they inspire me to do things, and the other way around.

"What we love so much is the work of the artists before us," Moal concludes. "I admire [Ford designer] E. T. 'Bob' Gregorie and Edsel Ford. We love their designs; that's art. And we like to put our twist on what they did, so we chop the tops and so forth. But the fact of the matter is, those designs, the lines, the reveals, are truly art. But they were constrained to become mass production designs that were practical and affordable. Now we can go back and make them better.

"But really," Moal reflects, "I hope we create something some day that is *that* good."

1932 FORD ROADSTER owned by Steve Moal

1932 FORD FIVE-WINDOW COUPE owned by George Poteet

1934 FORD ROADSTER owned by Eric Zausner

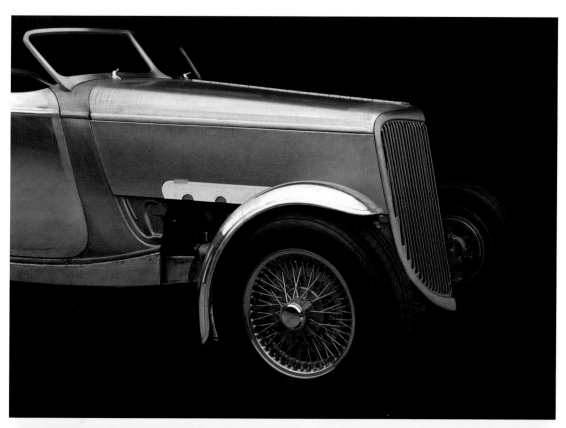

1941 CHRYSLER
AGHASSI ROYALE ROADSTER
owned by Hank Torian

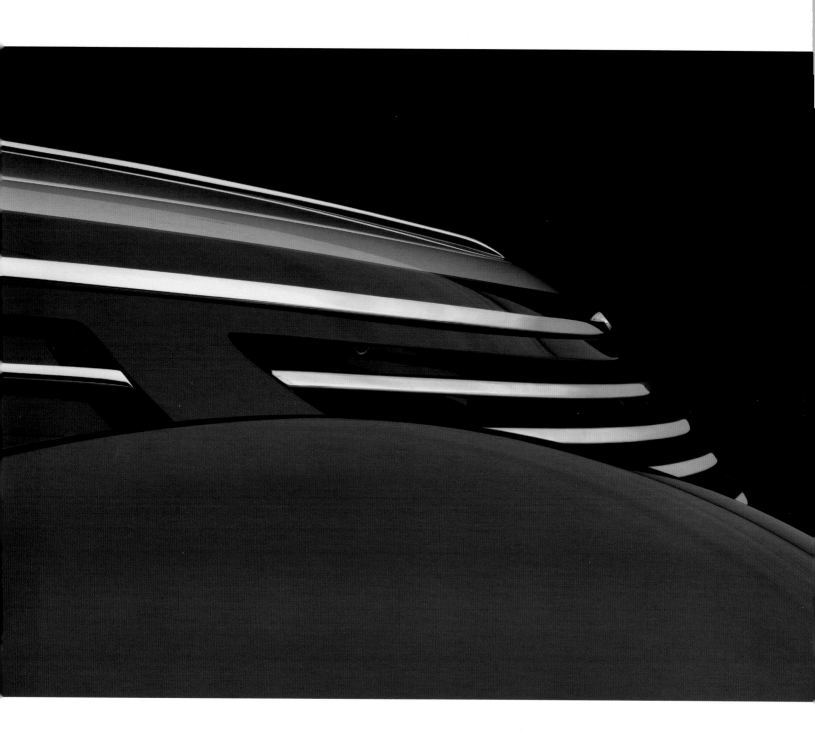

CHAPTER 19

ROY BRIZIO
Driven to Succeed

For years, Roy Brizio's crowded old shop in South San Francisco (now home to *The Rodder's Journal*) had numerous cars-in-progress stacked outside its cramped confines. After he moved a few miles away to larger premises, Brizio's shop is still crowded. But there's enough space so everything is done inside.

Brizio and his talented team (he calls it a team, not a crew) finish about half a dozen cars a month, including a couple of the crisp, clean-looking Deuce roadsters and coupes that have become his trademark. "We've probably done more '32s than any other professional shop," Brizio explains. "But we also build more cars than people realize." For the last 25 years, Roy Brizio Street Rods has been turning out an unending string of high-end, immaculately detailed hot rods of all shapes and sizes.

It started in the late '70s, not far from where Brizio's shop is located today. Brizio's father, Andy Brizio—a legend in his own right—was running Champion Speed Shop and had his own T-bucket fabrication business called Andy's Instant-T's. As a teenager, Roy spent hours fabricating chassis, working the Champion parts counter, and tweaking his own '32 three-window. As T-buckets faded from the scene, Andy needed more of Roy's time behind the counter. Seeking greener pastures, Roy started his own shop in nearby San Bruno. Initially, he was building hot rod chassis for Model As, Ts, and '32 Fords. By 1980 he moved to a location back in "South City," where he spent the next twenty-two years and established himself as one of the premier hot rod builders in the world.

Roy Brizio Street Rods doesn't seek the spotlight. Brizio will tell you, straight up, that he has absolutely no desire to take the big show awards that have increasingly captured the public eye in recent years. "I don't even want to do it," he says. "If a guy walked in and said 'Here's a million dollars, build me a Ridler-winning car,' that wouldn't motivate me. My guys would quit if I told them to go and hand-make every bolt.

"I go to the top shows and see those high-end cars. They're all beautiful, and every guy, whether it's the owner who made the money in the first place, or the fabricators and the team who made it happen—every one of those guys has worked so hard. But the problem with major awards is there's only one winner. Honestly, I'd rather see all those guys work to make ten cars that make ten people happy than to have seven out of eight [of the Ridler's Great Eight, for example] guys unhappy because they didn't win. That would create ten more cars that people would drive. I'd prefer to make ten people happy than one person unhappy."

You don't often hear a shop owner/businessman like Brizio talking about work he *doesn't* want to do, but buried in this honesty is the ethos that has made Brizio's business such a success. It's a three-tiered model, established over a quarter of a century: Build immaculate hot rods with careful attention to detail, infuse each car with timeless style, and make your customers happy.

"We have a reputation for building straightforward hot rods that are as simple as possible, yet they're very well-detailed, with plenty of power and good choices for wheels and tires. We nail our 'look' by painting cars in the right colors, with the right stance. We don't offer fully handmade suspensions, and we don't fabricate every single part. I appreciate the flathead-powered/quick-change-equipped nostalgia stuff, but that's not where most of my clientele are. I want to go down the freeway in the fast lane and shift gears. I want reliability."

Much of that innate reliability comes from Brizio's frequent use of modern V-8 powerplants. If a customer asks, he won't hesitate to install fully independent suspension, although that's not necessarily the preferred treatment in today's tradition-crazed hot rod community. "The nostalgia cars are great," says Brizio, "and I'd like everyone to have a historic car like that. But you can't always do it if it's your only car. We'll build you a new car that can look nostalgic. The '50s and '60s were my favorite years, and we build cars like those today, with late-model drivetrains. You can get in and drive them cross-country and never break down." Long a proponent of the Ford-in-a-Ford mindset, Brizio's shop has been doing a lot of business with Jack Roush, using new engines based on Ford engineering.

Almost anything goes, so long as his shop can fulfill a customer's wishes. Besides being adamant that his hot rods are meant to be driven, Brizio's built his business creating cars his customers have always wanted. "Usually, we'll do whatever a customer requests. In the '80s, we went the billet route a few times, and we weren't the best at that, but it's what people were asking for. If there's some element today where I want to throw in my two cents, I'm not shy about it. Sometimes we go my way and sometimes we won't. There are times when a car gets done and it isn't all my decision, it's the customer's. The best part about this business is doing it for people you like working for. They allow you to do this."

Perhaps the ultimate testimonial to Brizio's commitment to his clients is the heavy volume of repeat business his shop enjoys. From famous musicians and athletes to wealthy businessmen, it's not uncommon for a single hot rodder to come to Roy Brizio Street Rods two, five, or a dozen times. "Without my customers," Brizios says appreciatively, "I'd have simply been the guy in the two-car garage building roadsters for a hobby."

Not that Brizio sees anything wrong with that. While he's quick to praise several other professional builders around the country, especially the all-encompassing talent of Chip Foose and the recent work of Troy Trepanier and Eric Peratt, Brizio's pure enthusiasm for hot rodding finds him truly awed by do-it-yourselfers. "What really impresses me today is when I go to a car show or to a rod run and see a car that's truly bitchin', and the guy *built it in his garage*. I see stuff sometimes when I think, 'Can you imagine if this guy had equipment?' I mean, I've had guys walk into my shop with parts C-clamped together, asking me to weld it for them, and I don't even know what I'm looking at, and then they bring their cars here and I go, 'Sonofabitch built this car in his garage and he doesn't even have a *welder*, but he has a good eye and he knows how to work a file and a drill press.'"

Despite his almost anti-award bias, Brizio's team has taken the America's Most Beautiful Roadster trophy at the Grand National Roadster Show (Bay area–bred Brizio first attended "Oakland" when he was just a year old). He's begun researching and skillfully restoring historic hot rods and customs for long-time clients Jorge Zaragoza and John Mumford. Brizio's talented team, led by Bill Ganahl, restored the ex–Jack Calori '36 Ford coupe, a *Hot Rod* magazine cover car in 1949, and won the Historic Hot Rod Class at the Pebble Beach Concours d'Elegance in 2005. And a Brizio restoration of Tom McMullen's legendary *Deuce Roadster* captured third place in a tightly contested '32 Ford class at Pebble in 2007.

Admitting a small discrepancy there, Brizio muses, "Maybe it's a little unfair. I've had some great cars to build, so it's easier for me to have this attitude,

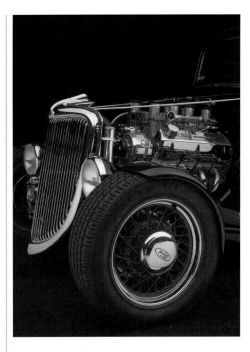

but honestly, I was never driven by the thought of winning awards. I certainly don't lay in bed at night thinking about someone bringing me a car to build to win at Oakland. I'm just fine. Instead, I lie in bed thinking, 'I hope someone brings me a bitchin' '32 three-window body so we can build him a cool car and make him happy.'"

Brizio sincerely appreciates the status he's earned as one of hot rodding's elite builders. "I'm far luckier than I ever dreamed of. I only ever cared about having a '32 Ford roadster, just one highboy with Halibrand wheels and a quick-change. The only thing I don't like about hot rodding is that the price of '32 Fords has gone up, and I can't buy as much stuff for myself. That's all I ever wanted, but I worked hard and here I am, with famous cars like the *Ala Kart* and the ex–Sam Barris Mercury in my shop, and with the Calori coupe and the McMullen roadster behind me." Brizio shakes his head, almost wistfully. "I think we're the luckiest shop in the country."

> ❝ *People ask if I still love what I do, and the answer is always, 'Yes, I do.' Sometimes when the shop is closed at night I just stop, look around, and think, 'God, we've done so much stuff.'* ❞

1933 FORD THREE-WINDOW COUPE owned by Jorge Zaragoza

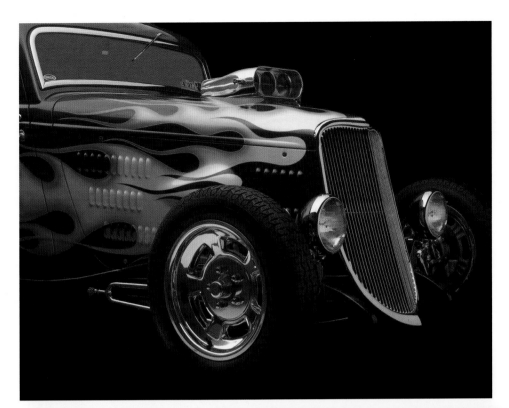

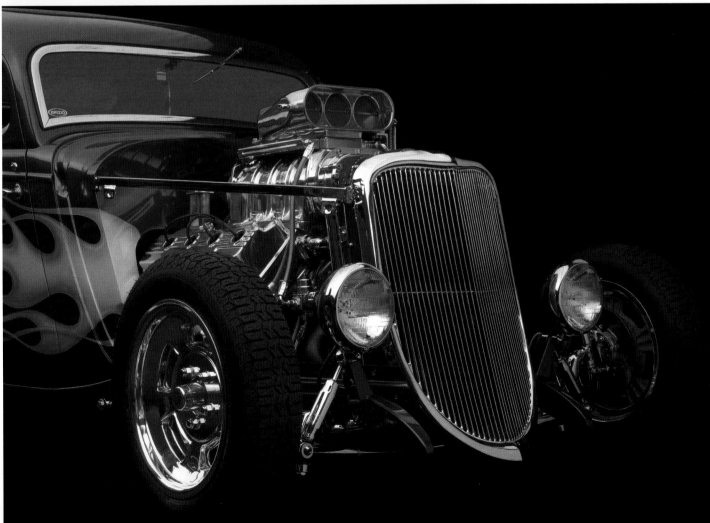

1932 FORD THREE-WINDOW COUPE owned by John Mumford

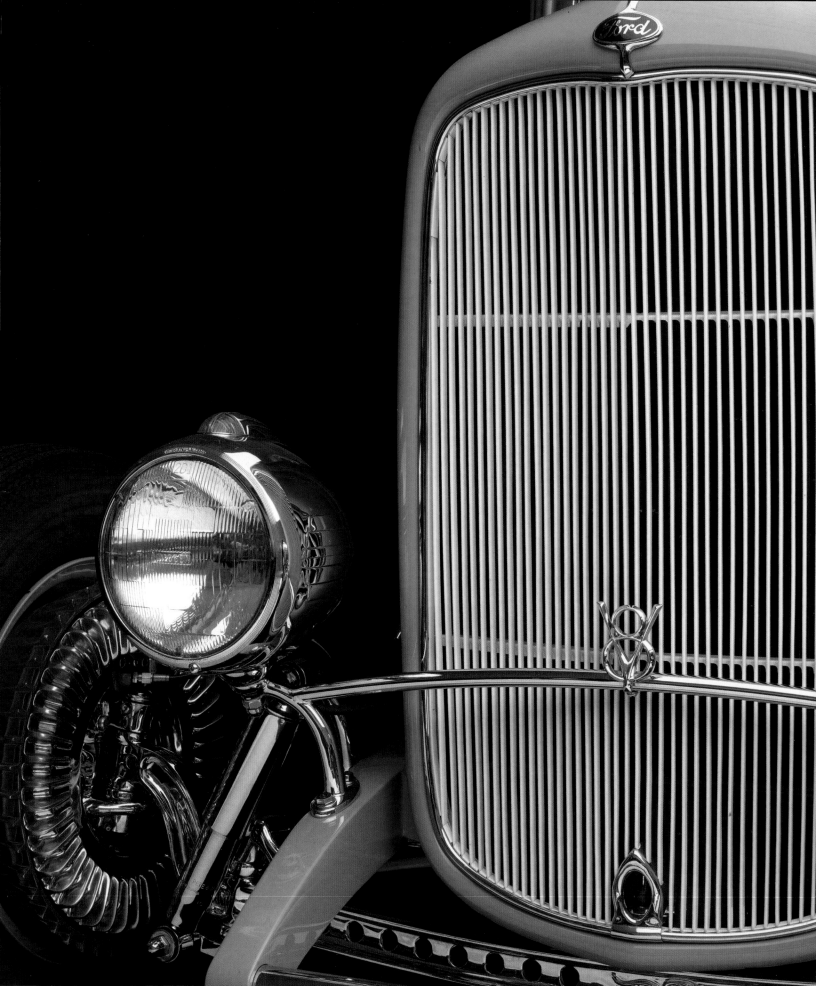

1929 FORD *ALA KART*
owned by John Mumford

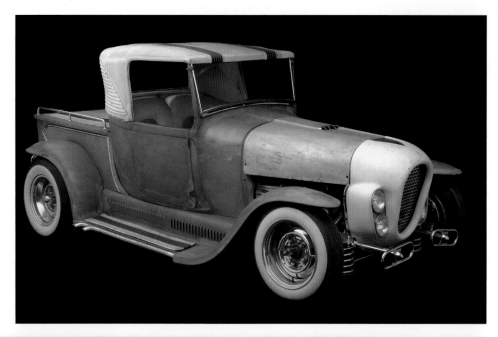

1934 FORD VICTORIA
owned by Paulette Zaragoza

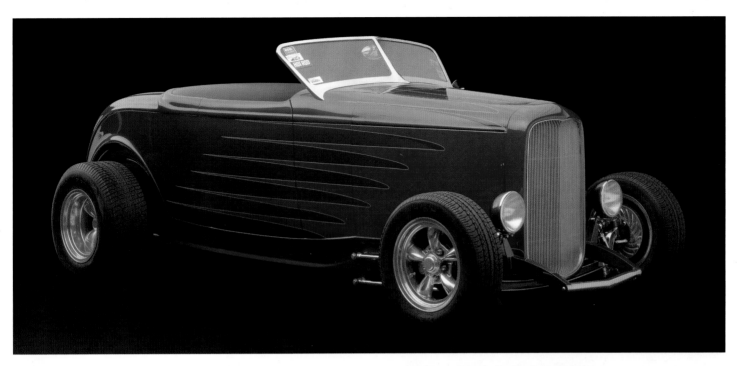

1932 FORD ROADSTER owned by Roy Brizio

1932 FORD ROADSTER owned by Roy Brizio

CHAPTER 20

VERN TARDEL
Time Warp

Vern Tardel is known for authentic Deuce high-boys that look as though they'd been hidden away since the '50s. He works out in the middle of nowhere. He's hard to communicate with (visitors are considered trespassers—you get the idea). He's working to keep aflame the dying light of the traditional hot rod.

Tardel's nature is contradictory. Is he a pioneering intellectual making the best of nostalgic technology, or a shortsighted mechanic who's stuck in 1955? He's been called a true artist, but Tardel himself derides the very *idea* that hot rods are art. Placed in a class by himself, he's never reached for the spotlight or a very tall trophy.

Tardel grew up in Santa Rosa, California, where his sprawling "Flathead Ranch" is located. Born in 1943 to a Merchant Marine machinist, young Tardel learned fabrication and auto mechanics. He was tasked with tending to the machinery that did the rough work on the family chicken farm/prune orchard. The Northern California hop-up scene caught his eye as well. "I was always around equipment," he recalls. "I picked up an interest in trucks and cars early on. The first car I built was in 1959. I finished it in '61. My dad was pretty liberal about me doing cars as long as I kept my homework up and didn't make a big mess. And I could drag stuff home if I kept it out of sight."

Tardel's progression from hobbyist to professional involved apprenticeships in brake and body shops, horse-trading of cars and parts, and a few body shops of his own, until he committed to full-time building hot rods. He ran flatheads, "always flat-heads," at the drags. "Chevys were pretty much dominant, but there was plenty of flathead hardware around. You could put some nitro in one of these motors. It'd last two races and then explode. Sometimes I won, but the motors wouldn't last because I'd be running so much nitro. I could break shit real easy with a 50 percent dose." After rodding, racing, and dis-assembling countless old Fords, Tardel accumulated a jaw-dropping parts collection; it's his resource for period-perfect hot rods.

A realist, Tardel will talk prospective customers out of his shop if they're blinded to the realities of early Ford motors. "The flathead is limited in cubic inches," he says in a surprisingly frank manner. "An overhead is more efficient and produces more power. A flathead won't breathe well because of its design. But I appreciate its simplicity. It's forgiving. When you put it together right, it runs dependably. You can get the spark plugs out without burning your hands. When you take the distributor off, you can look at the points and tell if it's going to work or not. When you look at electronic stuff there's a little magic box, you know? 'What's in there? I don't know. How's it work? I don't know.' I feel 'simple' is not necessarily the best, or the latest, but it's comfortable."

In the early 1990s, Tardel (already an old Bonneville hand) set his first salt flats record in a Nash Rambler (Ford flathead–powered, of course). The '32 roadster he campaigns with his son Keith is the XF/BFMR record holder, with a two-way average of 166.470 mph.

"I see [traditional roadsters] as my style, and also I'm a cheap son of a bitch," he jokes, as if he were just dipping in his remarkable parts stash over and over. Tardel's attention to detail and fundamental respect for the earliest hot rodders is his motivation. "I've always been able to take something that's laying around and make it work. That's the heart of the hot rod thing, early on. Guys would take what they could find and make it work, taking one part off a car and adapting it to another. After World War II, the guys that came back from the service or the ones in the aircraft industry had *good skills*; they'd been trained. And there were thousands of neat and cheap war surplus pieces—quality shit that'd make a car stand out or perform better.

"My style stems from my roots and experience with Ford hardware. I have a strong thing about preserving history. The thing I like about these cars is they're forgiving. Ford metal is really easy to work with . . . Henry [Ford] was a cheap shit too, but he bought a very good staff of engineers." He also used the best possible materials, like molybdenum steel, so they'd last and last.

Decades ago, Tardel decided he'd build hot-rod Deuce highboy frames just the way he needed them to be. Today, his chassis are assembled on a large jig in his shop. His own cross-members (most often) join reproduction rails. Then the rear end, wishbones, springs, and shocks all go together on his frame rack. Most of his Deuce bodies are Brookville reproductions, which, along with reproduction frame rails, might violate the *uber* historic mystique. But "modern bodies are almost perfect," Tardel says; the magic lies in the details."

"I have a pretty good amount of Ford wishbones, spring perches, original axles, rear end housings, transmission cases and all the little crap that really makes a car stand out. Guys try to emulate traditional cars, but it doesn't work without integrating the real stuff.

His astounding parts-and-pieces collection is part of the reason Tardel is sometimes seen as a recluse. But it's his eagerness to help that forced him to remain relatively hidden. His reputation as an expert builder and parts hoarder resulted in constant queries; his brain was picked for everything from technical know-how to the whereabouts of an elusive part that someone just had to have. "It got so bad," Tardel says, "I was in the office all the time messing with paperwork or on the phone. So I just pulled the plug and decided I'm gonna just build some cars." You can reach him by fax, and that's the way Tardel likes it. "Either I have ten hours a

day on the phone, or I can make all the hours I have in this hobby count. I dedicate every minute to making a car move forward."

Compounding the loner mystique was the demise of Tardel's "Flathead Camp," a small but hugely respected class where Tardel shared his wisdom directly. The state of California got wind of the program and "bureaucracy absolutely killed it," Tardel laments. Still wanting to share what he knows, Tardel has teamed with writer Mike Bishop for a series of excellent books that cover everything from early transmissions to the ground-up assembly of a Deuce highboy.

> ❝ *My style stems from my roots and experience with Ford hardware. I have a strong thing about preserving history. The thing I like about these cars is they're forgiving.* ❞

"Kustom Kulture" artists like the late Ed Roth and Von Dutch moved into the mainstream art world. Tardel has seen his road-going cars celebrated as artistic creations. The San Francisco Museum of Modern Art displayed "Real Hot Rods by Vern Tardel" in late 2002. It was a step forward for hot rodding to be acknowledged as an important part of American culture. Tardel himself constituted the minority. "I'm not buying into the whole 'art' thing. Early hot rodders wanted to haul ass. In World War II, these guys had been in life-or-death situations where danger was not a fucking problem. You could get in your hot rod, go fast, and get a thrill. It was a speed trip; it's not like a sculpture."

But he's a man of contradictions. "A lot of Ford stuff *is* art deco. When you put those pieces onto a car, it's like creating a piece of sculpture. But it's different. When I think of art, I think of maybe a custom car."

That pragmatic approach typifies the real Vern Tardel. He just wants to build a hot rod the way they used to be built. He'd like to spend hours guiding the next generation, but that activity cuts into his time actually making these cars happen.

Tardel will turn away a customer if he thinks he's unprepared for the realities of traditional hot rodding. He feels hot rodding's leap to popular culture, thanks to TV shows he calls a "disservice to the hot rod community," has created a new kind of rodder with more money than sense. "One of my criteria for doing a car," he explains, "is that guys need to know what they're up against. A lot of the guys who want these cars have absolutely no idea what they're stepping into. It doesn't ride like a street rod. It's not a Lexus. It's got old technology. It takes a bit of tolerance on a customer's part."

Tardel is frank when he forecasts the near-end of traditional hot rodding. He's one of the few to openly state that this practice isn't getting bigger, and that once the current generation of hot rodders passes on, it may "taper off."

"The younger guys that build cars will shine. But even with Brookville building new bodies, younger people don't relate to that." He points to his frequent trips to Infineon Raceway on drag night and the kids "with little Japanese cars, tweaking the engines with laptops." It's hot rodding, and it's not very different from the youth of the '40s moving to then-cheap Ford roadsters. To Tardel, the attachment to Japanese cars is "just another direction that it's going to go."

What's most striking about Tardel's shop isn't the hot rods he builds there, but the hardware that peppers the grounds. Scattered about are antique farming machines, cobbled together from whatever materials their long-gone builder had handy. There's a rototiller that uses Model A front axles as frame rails, drawing power from an ancient Ford 4-banger, and machines built from even more esoteric materials. They reflect Tardel's rural heritage. They are the reason he appreciates traditional hot rods so deeply.

"Hot rodders are thinkers. They look at something and go, 'What can I put on to make *this* do something else?'" Everybody wants to pick Tardel's brain about what it takes to build a traditional hot rod his way, what many see as "the right way." You don't need an enormous parts collection or 50 years of experience like Tardel has. Even if he doesn't count himself among their flock, the secret to working like Tardel does is to work like an artist. And *think* first.

1932 FORD ROADSTER owned by Randy and Chris Cannarozzi

FLATHEAD ENGINE ON TEST STAND

1932 CHASSIS PROJECT owned by David Zivot

1932 FORD ROADSTER owned by Joe and Elyn Fazio

1932 FORD MODEL A ROADSTER
owned by David di Falco

1929 FORD
MODEL A ROADSTER
owned by Jay West

1929 FORD MODEL A PHAETON
owned by Joe and Elyn Fazio

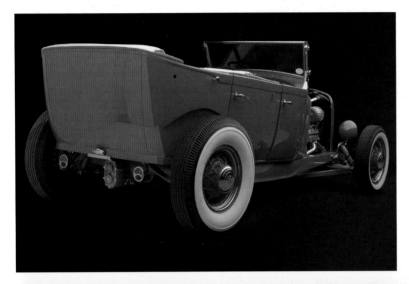

For *Art of the Hot Rod*, we planned to photograph more than one hundred cars from twenty builders spread across the entire country. The conventional approach would require renting studios in each area, maybe ten in this case, and transporting cars to the centralized sites. This approach was entirely possible, but it would have taken years and cost hundreds of thousands of dollars.

To streamline the process we needed a way to work quickly on each builder's site. To accomplish this, we built a self-contained mobile studio. It is based on a 28-foot fifth-wheel trailer. The 10-ft by 20-ft light bank is transported, assembled inside (hung from the roof on a trolley system), and in use is supported parallel to the side of the trailer by two arched trusses from the top. The height of the box is controlled remotely by linear actuators (screw jacks) at the back legs of the arches. The background is hung from a slotted extrusion (sailboat hardware) along the top edge. Don Schnieders, a race engineer of vast experience, collaborated in the conceptual stages, then designed and fabricated components.

The light source is an array of six to nine studio strobes mounted inside the light bank connected by cables to their individual power sources. They are triggered by a single radio transmitter mounted on the camera with a receiver on each power source. Photographing outside means that the artificial light has to overpower a lot of ambient light. We can use as much as 22,000 watt/second in order to underexpose direct sunlight.

The camera is a Hasselblad with a Hasselblad/Imacon digital back, hardwired through an image bank to a laptop or iMac computer. In case there is a terminal problem with the digital capture, I carry a conventional 4x5 view camera as backup.

The mobile studio worked well from the first day. During the tour we photographed more than one hundred cars at twenty-six sites and traveled 13,000 miles in one and a half laps of the country. All of the work was done during the summer of 2006.

INDEX